HARBRACE COLLEGE WORKBOOK

FORM 9C

Writing for the World of Work

Sheila Y. Graham

University of Tennessee

HARCOURT BRACE JOVANOVICH, INC.

New York   San Diego   Chicago   San Francisco   Atlanta
London   Sydney   Toronto

Contents

MECHANICS

PUNCTUATION

SPELLING AND DICTION

EFFECTIVE SENTENCES

EFFECTIVE WRITING

To the Instructor

Welcome to a workbook about work. This is not merely an alternative edition of the *Harbrace College Workbook;* it is a new edition that is aimed at students who are interested in reading about and learning to write effectively for the world of work.

Arrangement   As in all previous editions of the *Harbrace College Workbook,* the materials in Form 9C are arranged according to section number: Sections **1** through **32** in the *Workbook* parallel the first thirty-two sections of the *Harbrace College Handbook,* Ninth Edition. Section **33** in the *Workbook* corresponds to Section **34** in the *Handbook.* In Form 9C, Section **1** covers the main points of grammar and punctuation; it is, in other words, a practical minicourse in the grammar and punctuation of sentences. Some students may be able to move directly from Section **1** to the later sections that treat word choice and sentence effectiveness (Sections **20** through **30**) or even to the sections that go beyond the sentence to longer units of composition (**31** through **33**). Other students will need additional review of basis areas—such as agreement, tense, and the uses of the comma and apostrophe—that is supplied in the intervening sections (**2** through **19**). Of course, the needs of the class or the individual student will determine how much time is spent on Sections **2** through **19** and how many of the exercises in each section are assigned.

Exercises   The subject matter of the exercises is the world of work. The exercises cover such topics as the importance of work, job predictions and job descriptions for the next decade, preparation for an interview, types of speaking and writing required in a variety of careers, and work-related issues such as increased leisure time, early retirement, and part-time employment. There are many more exercises in Form 9C related to basic areas of grammar and punctuation than in other forms of the *Workbook,* so students should not run out of exercise material before they have mastered a specific skill. For example, there are nine exercises (four in Section **1** and five in Section **6**) related to agreement and fifteen exercises on the uses of the comma (six in Section **1**, six in Section **12/13**, and three in Section **17**). Twelve exercises in Form 9C stress the use of sentence-combining techniques to achieve an effective style.

Writing   Form 9C includes not only sections on writing paragraphs and essays but also a section (**33**) on the special kinds of composition needed in the world of work—for example, letters of application, letters of complaint, memorandums, and reports. New to Form 9C is a discussion of the documented report, with a sample paper on work in the year 2000. Students may draw on the ideas and facts presented in the *Workbook*'s discussions and exercises for help in writing their own compositions.

The Dictionary   Proper use of the dictionary is stressed throughout Form 9C: in the study of nouns, adjectives, adverbs, and verbs, and in the sections on capitalization, abbreviations, italics, and numbers. But unless each member of the class is familiar with the dictionary, the best place to begin teaching and learning dictionary skills is Section **19**, "Good Usage and the Dictionary."

Spelling   Although most students receive little formal instruction in spelling after elementary school, correct spelling is important to success in school, as well as in future careers. Form 9C does not presume to be a complete spelling manual, but it does emphasize throughout use of the dictionary to avoid various kinds of misspellings, and it does cover all major spelling rules. In addition, it presents a list of words that are frequently misspelled in technical writing. Perhaps even more important, the "Individual Spelling List" at the end of the *Workbook* offers a chart on which students can record the words they misspell in their writing assignments and the reasons for the misspellings.

Acknowledgments   The late John Hodges, my associate, friend, and teacher in the writing of textbooks, reminded me almost daily while we worked on Forms 5 and 6 that "a good book is not written but *re*written." I am grateful to many people for their guidance in the rewriting of Form 9C, most especially to my editors, Sidney Zimmerman and Andrea Haight, who directed the revision of both the manuscript and the page proof; the late William Pullin, my editor and friend for many years, who suggested the theme for the exercises in 9C as well as several other forms of the *Workbook;* and Drake Bush, Bob Beitcher, and Paul Nockleby—all editors who played a part in planning the manuscript for 9C. I also very much appreciate the careful work and imagination of Stephen O. Saxe, the designer of Form 9C, and Robert C. Karpen, the production manager of the Workbooks. In preparing this revision I have been helped particularly by the thorough critiques of Form 8C made by Barbara Stout, Montgomery College, and Stanley Kozikowski, Bryant College. Their suggestions led to a complete revision of Section **1**. Other reviewers who contributed valuable ideas to Form 9C include David Bloomstrand, Rock Valley College; Rex Burwell, Northern Illinois University; Stephen Reid, Colorado State University; and Lawrence Shinebarger, State University of New York Agricultural and Technical College at Alfred.

Sheila Y. Graham

To the Student

You learn how to write chiefly by correcting your own errors. Corrections made for you are of comparatively little value. Therefore your instructor points out the errors but allows you to make the actual revision for yourself. Your instructor usually indicates a necessary correction by a number (or a symbol) marked in the margin of the theme opposite the error. If a word is misspelled, the number **18** (or the symbol **sp**) will be used; if there is a sentence fragment, the number **2** (or the symbol **frag**); if there is a faulty reference of a pronoun, the number **28** (or the symbol **ref**). Consult the text (see the guides on the inside covers), master the principle underlying each correction, and make the necessary revisions. Draw one line through words to be deleted, but allow such words to remain legible in order that the instructor may compare the revised form with the original.

In certain cases your instructor may require that you pinpoint your errors by supplying the appropriate letter after the number written in the margin. For example, after the number **12** in the margin you should take special care to supply the appropriate letter (**a, b, c, d,** or **e**) from the explanatory sections on the comma to show why the comma is needed. Simply inserting a comma teaches little; understanding why it is required in a particular situation is a definite step toward mastery of the comma.

Specimen Paragraph from a Student Theme

Marked by the Instructor with Numbers

3   Taking photographs for newspapers is hard work, it is not

12 the romantic carefree adventure glorified in motion pictures and

18 novels. For every great moment recorded by the stareing eye of

the camera, there are twenty routine assignments that must be

28 handled in the same efficient manner. They must often overcome

24 great hardships. The work continues for long hours. It must meet

deadlines. At times they are called on to risk their lives to ob-

tain a picture. To the newspaper photographer, getting a good

2 picture being the most important task.

Marked by the Instructor with Symbols

cs   Taking photographs for newspapers is hard work, it is not

,/   the romantic carefree adventure glorified in motion pictures and

sp   novels. For every great moment recorded by the stareing eye of

    the camera, there are twenty routine assignments that must be

ref   handled in the same efficient manner. They must often overcome

    great hardships. The work continues for long hours. It must meet

sub   deadlines. At times they are called on to risk their lives to ob-

    tain a picture. To the newspaper photographer, getting a good

frag   picture being the most important task.

Corrected by the Student

3   Taking photographs for newspapers is hard work; it is not

12C   the romantic, carefree adventure glorified in motion pictures and

18   novels. For every great moment recorded by the ~~stareing~~ *staring* eye of

    the camera, there are twenty routine assignments that must be

28   handled in the same efficient manner. ~~They must often overcome~~ *Newspaper photographers must often overcome great hardships and work long*

24   ~~great hardships. The work continues for long hours. It must meet~~ *hours to meet deadlines.*

    ~~deadlines.~~ At times they are called on to risk their lives to ob-

    tain a picture. To the newspaper photographer, getting a good

2   picture ~~being~~ *is* the most important task.

Sentence Sense

1

Develop your sentence sense.

To see the need for sentence sense, read the following paragraph about careers, if possible both silently and aloud.

> A person has more than thirty-five thousand different kinds of careers to chose from most people try to choose their careers carefully because they know they will be working for most of their lives they want their careers to be meaningful to themselves and to others each person wants to choose a career that makes the best use of his or her interests and talents clearly the choice of a career is one of the most important and most difficult decisions one makes in life.

For this paragraph to have meaning, you must use your sentence sense to group words into separate units of thought. You may have to read the paragraph several times to understand the meaning because the writer has not used the periods and capital letters that show where one sentence ends and another begins. Therefore you, the reader, must supply the sentence clues like the ones in the following paragraph.

> A person has more than thirty-five thousand different kinds of careers to choose from. Most people try to choose their careers carefully. Because they know they will be working for most of their lives, they want their careers to be meaningful to themselves and to others. Each person wants to choose a career that makes the best use of his or her interests and talents. Clearly, the choice of a career is one of the most important and most difficult decisions one makes in life.

In writing *about* careers, only confusion may result from the writer's failure to follow a standard and accepted form that the reader clearly understands. But what about writing *for* a career? Imagine the harm that would be done if the writer wrote this kind of label for a pain-killing product:

> Take two tablets every four hours for relief of pain from muscular aches headache and toothache for no more than ten days do not exceed recommended dosage unless advised by a physician keep out of reach of small children if pain persists consult a physician.

In this case the reader's possible misunderstanding of where sentences begin and end could have serious results for both the producer of the product and the buyer. Whatever the career, the first duty of the writer is to follow a form that will be clear to those who read the writer's label or message.

Our plan for writing for the world of work begins with developing sentence sense.

1a Learn the three main parts of a sentence.

A sentence is made up of a subject and a predicate. The subject tells who or what the sentence is about, and the predicate says something about the subject.

Subject + Predicate

People + once had few choices in careers.

The predicate may be divided into two parts: the verb and the complement. The verb expresses an action, an occurrence, or a state of being. The complement completes the meaning of the verb, or it says something about the subject. From now on, the subject of the sentence will be underlined once; the verb, twice; and the complement, three times.

People once had few choices in careers. [*Had* is the verb; it expresses an occurrence. *Choices* is the complement; it completes the meaning of the verb (People had what? Few *choices*).]

The choices in careers were few. [*Were* is the verb; it expresses a state of being. *Few* is the complement; it says something about the subject (*few* choices).]

Not every sentence has a complement, though most do.

During the last century many new careers have opened up. [The verb, *has opened up*, has no complement.]

Order of Sentence Parts The usual order for the three main sentence parts is subject, verb, complement (S-V-C). But in most questions, in emphatic sentences, and in sentences beginning with *there*, the order of the sentence parts varies.

USUAL ORDER Today's world offers many careers.

QUESTION Have you investigated various career opportunities? [A part of the verb precedes the subject.]

EMPHATIC Many are the possibilities. [The subject comes last; the complement, first.]

THERE There are books about careers in the library. [The verb precedes the subject. There is no complement in a sentence beginning with *there*.]

The order of the main sentence parts is very important in a language like English because the function of a word often depends on its position in the sentence. In the examples below, *employer* is a subject in the first sentence and a complement in the second; on the other hand, *employees* is a complement in the first sentence and a subject in the second. Only the position of these two words tells you what part they play in the sentences.

The employer praised the employees.

The employees praised their employer.

Each of the three main sentence parts—subject, verb, complement—will be explored in depth in the following pages.

Main sentence parts   Exercise 1–1

NAME _____ SCORE _____

DIRECTIONS   In the following sentences, the subject is underlined once; the verb, twice; and the complement (when there is one), three times. If the main parts of the sentence are in the usual word order, write _1_ in the blank; if they vary from the usual order, write _2_ in the blank. When you have finished the exercise, answer the questions that follow it.

EXAMPLE
What would you have done to make a living during the 1700s?   _2_

1. Your career in colonial America would probably have been

   farming.   _1_

2. In the early days of our country most families farmed for a living.   _1_

3. Every member of the family had a job on the farm.   _1_

4. There were many chores to be done each day.   _2_

5. Families were, of necessity, quite large.   _1_

6. A few people in a community worked in a general store.   _1_

7. Have you seen a record book of one of these early stores?   _2_

8. A book in the Cades Cove Community of Tennessee shows the

   purchases of a typical family in the area.   _1_

9. What products did most families buy?   _2_

10. Typical purchases were things like tobacco, coal oil, coffee, and

    shoes.   _1_

11. Most families paid for their purchases with products from their

    farm.   _1_

12. During the 1800s the Agricultural Revolution spread to North

    America.   _1_

13. Fewer <u>people</u> <u>were</u> then <u>needed</u> on the farm. _____1_____

14. <u>Springing</u> up everywhere <u>were</u> <u>factories</u>. _____2_____

15. Many <u>people</u> <u>found</u> <u>jobs</u> of various types in the factories. _____1_____

QUESTIONS

1. How many sentences have the main parts arranged in the usual

   order? _____

2. Which sentence varies from usual order for the sake of emphasis? _____

3. How many sentences lack complements? _____

4. Rewrite sentence 7 in usual word order.

5. Rewrite sentence 14 in usual word order.

1b Use a verb in every sentence. Find the verb first when you look for sentence parts.

Every sentence has a verb, even the one-word sentences that trainers use to communicate with their dogs: *Stay. Heel. Fetch. Sit.*

Function   Like the words spoken by a dog trainer, most verbs express action. But other kinds of verbs express occurrences or states of being.

> ACTION   Most people now *work* eight hours a day.

> OCCURRENCE   Many people *choose* their careers during their teen-age years.

> STATE OF BEING Sometimes people *become* unhappy with their careers.

Note: The verb may appear as part of a contraction: I*'m* (I *am*), we*'re* (we *are*), he*'d* (he *had* or he *would*).

Sometimes a word looks like a verb because its meaning is associated with action, but it is functioning as some other sentence part—quite often as the subject or a modifier. Take the word *work*, for example, which is an action word but which may serve as a subject, a verb, or a modifier.

> SUBJECT   *Work* is important to most people.

> VERB   People *work* for reasons other than pay.

> MODIFIER   The five-day *work* week may become obsolete.

To distinguish between *work* as a verb and *work* as some other sentence part, try putting an article (*a, an,* or *the*) in front of the word; if the sentence still makes sense, then the word is probably functioning as some other sentence part, but if the sentence does not make sense with the article included, the word is functioning as a verb.

> SUBJECT   [*The*] Work is important to most people.

> VERB   People [*the*] work for reasons other than pay.

> MODIFIER   *The* five-day work week may become obsolete.

Transitive and Linking Verbs   Many verbs serve as transitive verbs; they pass their action along to the complement or complements. (See also **1c**.)

> TRANSITIVE   Fortunately, people can change their careers.   [Can change what?
>
> *Careers* receives the action of the verb.]

> TRANSITIVE   An internship showed me the need to change my career plans.
>
> [Showed whom what? *Me* and *need* receive the action of the verb.]

7

Other verbs—like *be, seem, appear,* and *feel*—link their subjects with complements that say something about the subjects. (See also **1c.**)

> LINKING   I was grateful for the internship program.   [*Was* links the subject with a complement, *grateful,* that says something about the subject.]

Helping Verbs   Often the main verb—which shows the action, occurrence, or state of being—is accompanied by one or more helping verbs—usually forms of *be* (*is, are, was, were, has been, have been, will be,* etc.) or *has, have, do, can,* or *could* (see the Appendix for a more complete list of helping verbs). The helping verb or verbs may come immediately before the main verb or may be separated from the main verb.

> Fortunately, people today *can change* their careers.   [The helping verb, *can,* immediately precedes the main verb, *change.*]
> They *do* not *have* to remain in the same career forever.   [The helping verb, *do,* is separated from the main verb, *have,* by *not.*]
> *Have* you *found* your career yet?   [The helping verb, *have,* is separated from the main verb, *found,* by the subject, *you.*]

Notice that a verb like *have, has, be, can,* and *do* work either as the main verb of the sentence or as a helping verb. In the second example above, *have* is the main verb; in the third example, it is the helping verb.

Note: The helping verb, like the main verb, may be a part of a contraction: *can*'t find (*can*not find), she*'s* coming (she *is* coming), we*'ve* gone (we *have* gone).

Particles   The main verb may also be accompanied by a word or words like *to, in, with, up,* and *of* that add to or change the meaning of the main verb.

> We *put* our names on the list of applicants for the job.   [main verb]
> We *cannot put up* much longer with the company's delay.   [The main verb, *put,* is accompanied by a helping verb, *can,* and a particle, *up.*]

Compound Verbs   Often a sentence has two verbs connected by *and, but, or,* or *nor.*

> We *applied for* summer work but *did* not *hear* from the company for a month.
> We *waited* and *waited* for some word.

Form   Verbs can change their form to show number (one or more) and tense (the time of the action, occurrence, or state of being). Singular verbs in the present tense usually end in *s* or *es*, and past tense verbs usually end in *d* or *ed*. (The dictionary shows all unusual changes in verb form.)

> A person usually *shows* a natural inclination to work with people or with things. [singular number; present tense]
> People *show* their preferences in many ways.   [plural number; present tense]
> She *has decided* on a career in counseling.   [past tense shown by *d* ending of main verb; singular number shown by helping verb, *has*]
> They *have selected* accounting as their major.   [past tense shown by *ed* ending of main verb; plural number shown by helping verb, *have*]

Functions of verbs   Exercise 1–2

NAME _____ SCORE _____

DIRECTIONS   The following famous quotations about work illustrate the various functions of verbs—to express action, occurrence, or state of being. The subject of each verb is already underlined once; you should underline each verb twice. (Most sentences have more than one verb.) Then make a list of the twenty-five verbs that you have located in these quotations.

EXAMPLE
Work is the refuge of people who have nothing better to do.
                                        —Oscar Wilde

1. Without work all life goes rotten.—Albert Camus

2. Like every man of sense and good feeling, I abominate work.—Aldous Huxley

3. I'm [I am] a great believer in luck, and I find the harder I work the more I have of it.—Thomas Jefferson

4. When a man tells you that he got rich through hard work, [you] ask him whose.—Don Marquis

5. You know what happens in the beehive? They kill those drones.—Congressman William Poage

6. Labor disgraces no man, but occasionally men disgrace labor.—Ulysses S. Grant

7. Apparently we all work for ourselves, but in reality we are always working for others.—Dr. William Stekhel

8. In the good old days when a man finished his day's work, he needed rest; nowadays he needs exercise.—Evan Esar

9. I never forget that work is a curse—which is why I've [I have] never made it a habit.—Blaise Cendrars

10. Most <u>people</u> like hard work. Particularly when <u>they</u> are paying for it.—

Franklin P. Jones

LIST OF VERBS

1.	14.
2.	15.
3.	16.
4.	17.
5.	18.
6.	19.
7.	20.
8.	21.
9.	22.
10.	23.
11.	24.
12.	25.
13.	

Helping verbs and particles

NAME _____ SCORE _____

DIRECTIONS   In the following sentences the main verbs are underlined twice.
Find the helping verbs and particles that go with these main verbs and also
underline them twice. Then write the entire verb or verbs in the blank.

EXAMPLE
People should study the job market and match up their skills with the avail-

able positions. _*should study , match up*_____

1. A person may hear about a job opening from a friend or acquaintance. _____

   _____

2. Sometimes one comes up with a job because of the help-wanted section of the

   newspaper. _____

3. A person can also find work through public or private employment agencies.

   _____

4. Public employment agencies do not charge for their services, but private

   agencies usually do ask for payment. _____

   _____

5. Once a job seeker hears about a good opening, he/she should contact the

   employer or personnel director immediately. _____

   _____

6. The applicant for the job may <u>write</u> a letter or <u>call</u> for an interview with the

   potential employer. _____

7. A letter of application should always be carefully <u>written</u>, for it does <u>give</u> the

   employer a first, and usually a lasting, impression of the job seeker._____

   _____

8. The letter of application should be <u>considered</u> a letter of introduction.

   _____

9. The applicant's name, reason for writing, and special skills are <u>pointed</u> out

   in the letter._____

10. The letter should <u>include</u> a request for an interview and should <u>give</u> the ad-

    dress and telephone number of the applicant. _____

    _____

Main verbs, helping verbs, and particles

Exercise 1–4

NAME _____ SCORE _____

DIRECTIONS   In the following sentences the subjects have been underlined once. Underline the complete verbs twice—that is, the main verbs and, if there are any, the helping verbs and particles. Some sentences have compound verbs. Write the complete verb or verbs for each sentence in the blank.

EXAMPLE
The applicant may send in a résumé with the letter of application.

may send in

1. Sometimes the résumé is taken to the interview rather than mailed in ahead of time. _____

2. A résumé explains in outline form the applicant's education, skills, and job experience. _____

3. A résumé is usually confined to one or two pages. _____

4. The name, address, and telephone number of the applicant normally lead off the résumé. _____

5. The educational record and employment background of the applicant, as well as certain personal information—age, sex, marital status—make up the body of the résumé. _____

6. The résumé also lists three to five references. _____

7. These references should know about the applicant's qualifications for the job._____

8. Have you ever written a résumé? _____

9. A résumé should be filled out and read over carefully by the applicant.

_____

10. Most applicants type their résumés and make additional copies to use in the

future. _____

Forms of verbs   Exercise 1–5

NAME _____ SCORE _____

DIRECTIONS   In each of the following sentences, one verb has been omitted. Fill in the blank with the present tense (present time) of the verb written in parentheses after the sentence. If you think that the subject, which is printed in italics, is plural, or more than one, then drop the *s* ending from the verb or change the form to *are*.

EXAMPLES

Most college *courses* ___*present*___ more theory than practice. (presents)

The *practice* ___*comes*___ with the job.   (comes)

1. *People* _____ their work in different ways.   (sees)

2. Some *people* _____ their careers are the most important part of their lives.   (thinks)

3. Other *people* _____ their families are more important than their jobs.   (feels)

4. Many *arguments* _____ over the importance of work. (occurs)

5. "Idle *hands* _____ the devil's workshop" is a familiar saying. (is)

6. Another well-known *expression* _____ "All work and no play makes Jack a dull boy."   (is)

7. One *person* _____ that work is a person's reason for being. (says)

8. Another *person* _____ that work is something a person does to make enough money to do the important things in life.   (claims)

9. The *importance* of work _____ on the individual's values. (depends)

10. Still, most *people* _____ many hours a day at work. (spends)

11. *Workaholics* _____ it difficult to quit working.   (finds)

12. The *workaholic* _____ on at the office long after the end of the eight-hour day.   (stays)

13. Such a *person* rarely _____ a vacation.   (enjoys)

14. The workaholic's *characteristics* _____ inability to accept failure, guilt about level of productivity, and almost constant worry about performance.   (includes)

15. For the workaholic, all human *relationships* and leisure *activities* _____ unimportant when measured against success at work. (becomes)

16. There _____ more *workaholics* than most of us realize. (is)

17. Most *workaholics* _____ before they reach retirement age. (dies)

18. *Heart attacks* among workaholics _____ extremely common.   (is)

19. Of course, for every one workaholic there _____ at least one hundred lazy and incompetent *workers*.   (is)

20. Most *people* in the work force _____ somewhere between the two extremes.   (falls)

Verbals   Like verbs, verbals express action, occurrence, or a state of being. And they have endings—*ing, ed,* and *en*—that are the same endings verbs may have. Here, for example, are four verbal forms for the verb *take:*

>   *taking, taken, having taken, to take*

(Notice that *taking* and *taken,* when accompanied by helping verbs, are true verbs: *are taking* and *have taken,* for example.)

Finally, like verbs, verbals are often followed by words that complete their meaning.

> *Taking* my **time,** I found just the job I wanted.   [Taking what? *Time* completes the meaning of the verbal.]
> *Having taken* a vocational aptitude **test,** I was better able *to plan* a **career.**   [Having taken what? *Test* completes the meaning of the first verbal. To plan what? *Career* completes the meaning of the second verbal.]

But in spite of its similarities to a true verb, a verbal cannot serve as the verb of a sentence. Consider, for example, this sentence with its verb *have taken.*

> We have taken our time.

Notice that when a verbal replaces the verb, the word group is no longer a sentence. (See also **2a.**)

> we *taking* our time
> we *having taken* our time
> we *to take* our time

Thus whenever there is a verbal (or verbals) in a sentence, there must also be a main, or true, verb.

> *Taking* our time, we filled out the application carefully.

> *Having taken* our time, we answered each question completely.

> *To take* our time, we carried our applications home *to fill out.*

Recognizing verbs and verbals   Exercise 1–6

NAME _____ SCORE _____

DIRECTIONS   Here are ten famous quotations about work. The verbals have been printed in italics. Find the true verbs and underline them twice. In the first blank, write the verbal or verbals; in the second, write the verb or verbs.

EXAMPLE
I go on *working* for the same reason that a hen goes on *laying* eggs.—H. L.

Mencken

working, laying   go on, goes on

1. *Working* with people is difficult, but not impossible.—Peter Drucker

   _____   _____

2. We work *to become*, not *to acquire*.—Elbert Hubbard

   _____   _____

3. Work expands so as *to fill* the time available for its completion.—Northcote

   Parkinson

   _____   _____

4. Anyone can do any amount of work *provided* it isn't the work he is supposed

   to be doing at that moment.—Robert Benchley

   _____   _____

5. No man is obliged *to do* as much as he can do; a man is *to have* part of his life to

   himself.—Samuel Johnson

   _____   _____

6. Many men are hard workers: they're always looking around *to find*

   something for others *to do.*—Evan Esar

   _____ _____

7. Next to *doing* a good job yourself the greatest joy is in *having* someone

   else do a first-class job under your direction.—William Feather

   _____ _____

8. All the best work is done the way ants do things—by tiny but *untiring* and

   regular additions.—Lafcadio Hearn

   _____ _____

9. A great many people have . . . asked how I manage *to get* so much work *done*

   and still keep *looking* so *dissipated.*—Robert Benchley

   _____ _____

10. If there is one thing better than the thrill of *looking* forward, it is the ex-

    hilaration that follows the *finishing* of a long and *exacting* piece of

    work.—Alec Waugh

    _____ _____

1c Write a subject for every sentence except a command. Ask the verb "who?" or "what?" to find the subject of a sentence.

A sentence that has a verb but no stated subject is a command. In a command the subject is understood to be *you*, though it is not actually written down.

[You] Fill out the application form and return it to the personnel director.

In all other kinds of sentences, the subject is written down, even in the shortest of sentences.

Jesus wept.   [the shortest sentence in the Bible]

Function   The subject is who or what the sentence is about. Once you have located the verb in a sentence, all you need to do then is to ask who or what is *doing*, *occurring*, or *being*. Your answer will be the complete subject. To find the simple subject, ask specifically who or what the verb is talking about.

Many important values are derived from work.   [What are derived? Many impor-

tant values. What specifically are derived? Not "many important" but *values*.]

One of my friends desires a high income more than anything else.   [Who

desires? One of my friends. Who specifically desires? Not "of my friends,"

but *one*.]

It is important to be able to find the simple subject in a sentence so that you can make the number of the verb and the subject the same. If you mistake "friends" as the subject of the last example above, you will probably make the verb plural—"desire"—and thus make an error in agreement because the simple subject is *one* and the verb must be singular (*desires*) to agree with it in number. (See also Section **6**.)

Compound Subjects   Like the verb, a sentence may have more than one simple subject. The parts of the compound subject are connected by a word like *and*, *but*, *or*, or *nor* (printed in boldface below).

Income, recognition, **and** *adventure* are three goals sought by workers.
Not *income* **but** *adventure* is my main concern now.

Noun Subjects   A majority of simple subjects are nouns, words that name persons, places, things, and ideas. Since people first appeared on the earth, they have been interested in nouns. We are told that the first job Adam had was to name the things he saw in the Garden of Eden. We can imagine the fun he had pointing his finger at things and naming them: *sky, tree, bird, flower, apple, snake.* (Adam's name, of course, was a noun, too, as was the name of his mate, Eve.)

Modern people are still giving names to things. As soon as something new comes along, we rush to give it a name: *sputnik, astronaut, détente, rock and roll, Amtrak.*

Types of Nouns   Proper nouns begin with capital letters and name particular people, places, things, and ideas: *Columbus, New World, Mayflower, Thanksgiving, Declaration of Independence.* Common nouns are not capitalized; they are everyday names for general classes of people, places, things, and ideas: *explorer, continent, ship, holiday, capitalism.* Both common and proper nouns are often made up of more than one word: *home town, mother-in-law, oil well, Holy City, Bill of Rights.*

Many nouns name things that can be touched; these are called concrete nouns: *bread, house, kangaroo, glasses, trash.* Other nouns refer to matters that cannot be touched; these are called abstract nouns: *lesson, threat, plan, satisfaction, safety.*

As you can see, we need nouns to say almost anything, even to speak a nonsense sentence like "*Peter Piper* picked a *peck* of pickled *peppers.*"

Noun Signals   Certain words signal that a noun is coming. Both articles (*a, an, the*) and possessive pronouns (*my, your, his, her, its, our,* and *their*) are followed by nouns.

> The *Registrar* gave us **a** *copy* of **our** college *transcript.*

Form   Nouns change their endings to show two things: plural number and possession. When we name more than one of anything, we usually add an *s* or *es* to show that the noun is plural. (Remember that verbs act in just the opposite way: an *s* or *es* ending means that the verb is singular.)

> I have one job; Ethan has two jobs.
> I have one potato; Ethan has two potatoes.
> I love one woman; Ethan loves two women.
> I have one brother-in-law; Ethan has two brothers-in-law.   [Note that the chief word, *brother*, shows the sign of the plural.]

The dictionary shows you the plural for all nouns that form their plurals in some way other than the addition of *s* (for example, *man* → *men.*)

Singular nouns add an apostrophe and an *s* ('*s*) to show possession, or ownership. The possessive noun is placed in front of the person, place, thing, or idea possessed; in other words, we do not write *Ethan job* or *Ethan house* or *Ethan women.* Instead we write:

Ethan's job	Tony's frankness	Bess's kindness
Ethan's house	Tony's ideas	Bess's jeans
Ethan's women	Tony's parents	Bess's husband

The '*s* shows that Ethan, Tony, and Bess are possessive nouns.

If the possessive noun is plural, we usually add only the apostrophe:

jobs' requirements	teachers' salaries	guests' arrival
potatoes' roots	cities' problems	wolves' howling

But if the plural of the noun does not end in *s* (*women*, *children*, and *alumni*, for example), we add *'s* to form the plural possessive:

women's rights   children's absences   alumni's contributions

When a compound noun is made possessive, the last word shows the sign of the possessive case:

sons-in-law's jobs   the King of England's biography

Note: When we give a noun the possessive form, whether singular or plural, we change it to a modifier, a descriptive or qualifying word. (You will study modifiers in **1f**.)

Recognizing nouns

Exercise 1–7

NAME _____ SCORE _____

DIRECTIONS   Use *a*, *an*, and *the* to decide which of the following words are nouns: if a word sounds right with *a*, *an*, or *the* in front of it, write its plural form in the blank. If it does not, the word is not a noun; in that case, leave the blank empty. (If you are uncertain how to make the plural of the noun, consult your dictionary. When no plural form is given, the noun forms its plural in the usual way—by adding an *s* or *es*. See also **18f**.)

EXAMPLES

joke _____*jokes*_____

upon _____

1. boy _____

2. happy _____

3. on _____

4. book _____

5. light _____

6. time _____

7. with _____

8. slowly _____

9. reason _____

10. hobby _____

11. some _____

12. object _____

13. man _____

14. tomato _____

15. dollar _____

16. believe _____

17. belief _____

18. territory _____

19. rank _____

20. such _____

21. loss _____

22. sister-

in-law _____

23. shelf _____

24. cupful _____

25. big _____

DIRECTIONS   Use a possessive pronoun—*our,* for example—to decide which of the following words are nouns. If a word sounds right with *our* in front of it, write its plural in the blank. If it does not sound right with *our* in front of it, leave the blank empty because the word is not a noun. Use your dictionary to help you form the plurals of nouns that do not follow the usual pattern of adding *s* or *es.*

1. radio _____

2. receive _____

3. porch _____

4. crisis _____

5. industry _____

6. fulfill _____

7. bus _____

8. carefully _____

9. mosquito _____

10. ox _____

11. cloth _____

12. artist-in-

    residence _____

13. separate _____

14. strategy _____

15. until _____

16. them _____

17. mother-

    in-law _____

18. tendency _____

19. cargo _____

20. valley _____

21. decide _____

22. church _____

23. monkey _____

24. excellent _____

25. joy _____

Making nouns possessive

NAME _____ SCORE _____

DIRECTIONS   Rewrite each of the following word groups so that the second noun is placed in front of the first one. Give the possessive form to the noun you placed first. (Remember that by making the noun possessive, you change it to a modifier.)

EXAMPLES

values of a person   *a person's values*

benefits of jobs   *jobs' benefits*

1. the complaint of a customer _____

2. interests of an applicant _____

3. goals of people _____

4. choices of a student _____

5. location of a company _____

6. training of the workers _____

7. addresses of employers _____

8. entrance to the building _____

9. office of the personnel director _____

10. experiences of the workmen _____

11. ideas of experts _____

12. experiment of the scientist _____

13. routes of bus drivers _____

14. board room of the officers of Xerox _____

15. arrangements by florists _____

16. letters of secretaries _____

17. results of the test _____

18. work of the cooks _____

19. concern of laboratory technologists _____

20. quarrels of the daughters-in-law _____

21. poetry of John Keats _____

22. plans of the agriculture

   commissioner _____

23. discussion of the employees _____

24. books belonging to Susan _____

25. grades of the students _____

Recognizing simple subjects

Exercise 1–9

NAME _____ SCORE _____

DIRECTIONS   The complete subject in each of the following sentences is italicized. Find the simple subject that tells specifically who or what the verb (underlined twice) is speaking about. Underline the simple subject with one line and write it in the blank. (Remember that a sentence may have a compound simple subject.)

EXAMPLES

A scowling woman slouched into the office.   *woman*

Her résumé, with its many typographical errors, was difficult to read.   *résumé*

1. *The woman's faded jeans* were not appropriate dress for an interview.   _____

2. *Neither her application nor her résumé* was neat.   _____

3. *The woman's lack of preparation for the interview* did not favorably impress the personnel director.   _____

4. *Her answers to the questions asked by the personnel director* were vague and halting.   _____

5. *The main requirements for the job that the woman sought* were neatness and self-confidence.   _____

6. *The interview with the personnel director* did not last long.   _____

7. Needless to say, *this inappropriately dressed and poorly prepared applicant* did not get the job.   _____

8. *The decision about who is hired for a given job* often depends on small details.   _____

9. *Many well-qualified people* <u>may apply</u> for a job. _____

10. *The person who really wants a job* <u>must prepare</u> carefully for the interview. _____

11. *Various procedures for preparing for an interview* <u>may be</u> helpful. _____

12. *One thing that the applicant might do* <u>is</u> to write out an autobiography. _____

13. *The details recorded in the autobiography* usually <u>furnish</u> answers to questions one may be asked. _____

14. *The interests and abilities of the applicant* <u>come out</u> in the autobiography. _____

15. *These two important areas* <u>are</u> usually <u>covered</u> during an interview. _____

16. *Another way to prepare for an interview* <u>is</u> to make a list of questions the interviewer might ask. _____

17. *The time spent in thinking through answers to these questions* <u>is</u> always worthwhile. _____

18. *Some especially well-prepared applicants* <u>have</u> actually <u>staged</u> mock interviews. _____

19. *The self-confidence and fluency gained by advanced preparation* <u>help</u> any applicant. _____

20. *A neatly filled-out application, a carefully typed résumé, and an attractive appearance* <u>are</u> three decided assets for any applicant. _____

32

Mastering noun subjects and verbs Exercise 1–10

NAME _____ SCORE _____

DIRECTIONS   Rewrite the subject and verb parts of the following sentences, changing the simple subjects and verbs from singular to plural. Underline the plural subjects with one line and the plural verbs with two lines.

EXAMPLE
A person trains for a job in various ways.

People (or Persons) train for

1. A student learns skills (for example, typing and bookkeeping) through high-school and college courses.

2. A course sometimes requires outside work in the field of the student's intended occupation.

3. For example, a would-be teacher does student teaching during the last year of college.

4. A prospective air-conditioning mechanic also serves an apprenticeship.

5. The experience in the field helps the trainee to understand the occupation.

6. Sometimes a trainee decides to change careers on the basis of experience in the field.

7. Other times an apprenticeship convinces a trainee to continue with his or her chosen career.

8. A summer job gives the student further training in a specialized occupation.

9. A summer position often pays little or nothing at all, but gives valuable experience.

10. Hence the trainee is rewarded in many ways.

Pronoun Subjects   The other common type of simple subject is the pronoun. The use of pronouns prevents the unpleasant repetition of nouns. Tarzan, the jungle hero, did not know about pronouns; he repeated the same nouns again and again.

> *Tarzan* rescues *Jane.*
> *Tarzan* falls in love with *Jane.*
> *Tarzan* takes *Jane* to *Tarzan's* tree house.

Clearly, Tarzan's speech would have been much improved if he had used pronouns—words that substitute for nouns.

> Tarzan rescues Jane.
> *He* falls in love with *her.*
> *He* takes *her* to *his* tree house.

Function   Pronouns replace nouns. They have no meaning other than the meaning of the nouns they substitute for. Notice that you do not know what is being discussed when the nouns that pronouns stand for are not made clear.

> VAGUE   *They* told *us* that *it* would have to be changed. *Some* thought *this* should be done; *others* thought *that* was needed.

The meaning of a pronoun is clear only when the reader is sure what noun is being replaced.

> NOUNS   All graduating *seniors* must take a one-hour *course* in "How to Get a Job."

> PRONOUNS   *They* must take *it* so that *they* will be prepared for job interviews.   [*They* replaces seniors; *it* replaces *course.*]

Types of Pronouns   Unlike the almost limitless number of nouns, there are only a certain number of pronouns. The most frequently used ones are called personal pronouns: *I, me, you, he, him, she, her, it, we, us, they,* and *them.* As their name indicates, these pronouns refer to people or to living things.

Other pronouns refer only to things: *something, nothing, everything,* and *which,* for example. A few pronouns can refer to either persons or to things: *everyone, one, each, most, some, many, all, both,* and *that.*

A few important pronouns that you will study in depth later—*who, whom, which, that, what, whose, whoever,* and *whomever*—help to expand sentences. These pronouns sometimes serve as the subjects of their own word clusters; and they, too, like all other pronouns, take their meaning from the nouns that they replace.

> The students *who* take this course are well prepared for their job interviews.   [*Who* is the subject of the verb *take;* it replaces the noun *students.*]
> This course, *which* is offered several times a semester, is invaluable to students. [*Which* is the subject of the verb *is offered;* it replaces the noun *course.*]

These same pronouns may be used to ask questions—and are called interrogative pronouns when they are so used.

> *Who* is your supervisor?
> *What* is your job?

Form   Unlike nouns, pronouns do not form their plural by adding *s* or *es;* instead, *I* becomes *we; he, she,* and *it* become *they.* One personal pronoun does not change form at all to show plural number—*you.* Other pronouns can be only singular or plural in number: for example, *each, one, both,* and *many.*

A few pronouns, like nouns, do form their possessive by adding an *'s:* someone's hat, everyone's concern, anyone's hope. All personal pronouns, however, have a distinct form for the possessive case; *my, mine, your, his, her, hers, its, our,* and *their.* And personal pronouns, unlike nouns, change their form to show whether they are being used as subjects or as objects of verbs (receivers of the action of the verbs).

SUBJECT   *He* lent his friend five dollars for lunch.

OBJECT   The friend gave *him* his money back the next day.

Pronouns as replacements for nouns   Exercise 1–11

NAME _____ SCORE _____

DIRECTIONS   The following paragraph, adapted from Studs Terkel's *Working,*[*] shows how repetitious our writing would be without pronouns. Above each underlined noun subject (which is sometimes accompanied by a modifier) write a pronoun that fits smoothly into the sentence.

As a child Vincent Maher dreamed of being a policeman. Vincent Maher tried

other jobs, but other jobs did not satisfy him. Vincent Maher was cut out to be

a policeman, and Vincent Maher finally became one. Police work totally satis-

fied him. Police work made him feel necessary to people even though people often

ridiculed him. People called him a bigot and a hypocrite, but Maher saw himself

only as a human being with a job to do. Vincent Maher tried not to judge people

as superficially as people judged him. Maher preferred to work in poor neigh-

borhoods because the people there especially needed him. In white middle-class

neighborhoods Maher was expected to write parking tickets and scold people

when their dogs defecated on the grass. Maher did not become a policeman to do

this kind of work. All his life Maher worked compulsively, both during and after

hours, to become a detective. But being a detective was a goal he never achieved.

_____

[*] Studs Terkel, *Working: People Talk About What They Do All Day and How They Feel About What They Do* (New York: Avon Books, 1975), pp. 183–201.

Recognizing pronoun subjects

NAME _____ SCORE _____

DIRECTIONS   The verbs in the following sentences have been underlined twice. Underline all subjects with one line, and write the pronoun subjects in the blanks. Most sentences have more than one subject.

EXAMPLE
The jobs that require writing skills are many.   _that_

1. Who needs writing skills?   _____

2. Virtually everyone must do some writing.   _____

3. You and I will probably have desk jobs.   _____

4. That means writing reports, letters, and memos.   _____

5. Some careers that are very different from so-called

   desk jobs also require writing skills.   _____

6. An electrician, who may spend the night working on

   power lines broken during a storm, must fill out a report

   at the end of the job.   _____

7. Hardly anyone today escapes the job of writing.   _____

8. My husband, who is a microbiologist, does more writing

   than I do as a textbook author.   _____

9. As often as not, the writing skills of the applicants deter-

   mine who gets a particular job.   _____

10. Also, one is often promoted on the basis of ability to han-

    dle paper work effectively.   _____

Mastering subjects: a review   Exercise 1–13

NAME _____ SCORE _____

DIRECTIONS   All verbs in the following sentences are underlined twice. You are to underline once the noun or pronoun subjects that tell who or what is doing, occurring, or being. Then in the first blank write the subject, and in the second blank write the verb. (Remember that a sentence may have a compound subject and/or verb.)

EXAMPLE
Studs Terkel's *Working* was a best seller in the early 1970s.

_____*Working*_____   _____*was*_____

1. Terkel's book gives us a different way of looking at life in the twentieth

   century.   _____   _____

2. This book shows people's attitudes toward their jobs.

   _____   _____

3. The people interviewed by Terkel speak honestly and straightforwardly

   about their jobs. _____   _____

4. Everyone interviewed by Terkel has strong feelings about his or her work.

   _____   _____

5. Some of the workers feel fulfillment in their jobs.

   _____   _____

6. Others simply endure their jobs in order to live.

   _____   _____

7. Terkel interviewed all kinds of people.

   _____   _____

8. Both blue-collar and white-collar workers speak out in Terkel's book.

   _____   _____

9. Even a prostitute has her say in *Working*.

   _____ _____

10. Terkel's interviewees are all searching for meaning in life.

   _____ _____

11. They want to be remembered for something.

   _____ _____

12. Some find a kind of immortality through their work.

   _____ _____

13. Many, though, simply survive their workdays.

   _____ _____

14. There are more unhappy workers than happy workers.

   _____ _____

15. Does this fact surprise you?

   _____ _____

16. Or are you also pessimistic about satisfaction being provided by work?

   _____ _____

17. The unhappy workers in Terkel's book view themselves as machines or ob-

    jects.   _____ _____

18. Usually included in their descriptions of their roles is the word *robot*.

   _____ _____

19. A few of the workers take pride in their jobs.

   _____ _____

20. A bookbinder and a fireman both speak of the satisfaction of saving some-

    thing.   _____ _____

Mastering subjects and verbs: a review Exercise 1–14

NAME _____ SCORE _____

DIRECTIONS Underline the noun or pronoun subjects with one line, the verbs with two lines. (Remember to look first for the verbs in the sentences.) Then write the subject in the first blank and the verb in the second.

EXAMPLE
Our country is supposedly built on the work ethic.

_____*country*_____   _____*is built*_____

1. The Bible speaks of Adam and Eve's expulsion from the Garden of Eden.

   _____   _____

2. A punishment for their disobedience was to earn their bread by the sweat of

   their brows.   _____   _____

3. The idea of work has seldom been questioned in our history.

   _____   _____

4. But some people today are questioning the importance of work.

   _____   _____

5. Should a person really find fulfillment in work?

   _____   _____

6. The discontent of workers with their lot takes many forms.

   _____   _____

7. Slovenly work is one outlet for discontent.

   _____   _____

8. Another is a put-down of the importance of craftsmanship.

   _____   _____

9. The amount produced becomes more important than the quality of the pro-

   duction.   _____   _____

10. There are still other symptoms of workers' dissatisfaction with their lot.

_____ _____

11. Excessive absenteeism and tension often result from workers' unhappiness with their jobs. _____ _____

12. Managers and employees alike are evaluating their jobs and finding them un-fulfilling. _____ _____

13. Is it then a person's lot to be unhappy with his or her job?

_____ _____

14. Or should people search harder to find meaningful jobs for themselves?

_____ _____

15. Should American workers rededicate themselves to finding satisfaction in and respect for their work?

_____ _____

16. No one can give an answer to these questions for someone else.

_____ _____

17. However, Terkel's book does clearly show the widespread concern of the American people about the meaning of their jobs.

_____ _____

18. Perhaps the questioning of the work ethic will produce positive results.

_____ _____

1d Ask the subject and verb "who?" or "what?" to find the complement of a sentence.

If you receive an answer when you follow the subject and verb with "who?" or "what?" the sentence has a complement or complements.

NO COMPLEMENT   Our workday ends at 4:30.   [Workday ends who or what? There is no answer in the sentence. The words that follow the verb answer a different question—"when?"]

COMPLEMENT   We are happy with our schedule.   [We are what? *Happy.*]

COMPLEMENTS   Our schedule gives us a head start on the afternoon traffic.   [Our schedule gives who? *Us.* Gives us what? A *head start.*]

Objects   Transitive verbs transfer or pass their action along to a complement or complements. The words affected by or acted upon by transitive verbs are called objects. A verb like *give*, *buy*, *send*, *call*, *consider*, and *find* have more than one object.

OBJECT   My supervisor, Mr. Tom McMahon, manages twenty employees in our laboratory.   [The object, *employees*, shows whom the verb, *manager*, is acting upon. It it called the direct object.]

OBJECTS   He gives us careful instructions for each experiment.   [The first object, *us*, shows to whom or for whom something is being done. It is called the indirect object.]

OBJECTS   We find his instructions helpful.   [The second object, *helpful*, describes something about the direct object, *instructions*. It is called the object complement.]

Subject Complement   Linking verbs—mainly forms of *be* (*am*, *is*, *are*, *was*, *were*, *has been*, *have been*, *will be*, etc.) and verbs like *appear*, *seem*, *look*, *feel*, and *taste*—are followed by complements that describe or show something about the subject. These complements are called subject complements.

SUBJECT COMPLEMENT   Mr. McMahon has been my supervisor for five years.   [The noun *supervisor* shows something about the subject. It is sometimes referred to as a predicate noun or the predicate nominative.]

SUBJECT COMPLEMENTS   He is strict but considerate.   [*Strict* and *considerate* describe the subject. They are called predicate adjectives.]

Often you must be able to pick out the exact complement or complements in the sentence to avoid mistakes in the form of the pronoun or the modifier. (See also Sections **4** and **5**.)

> The supervisor gives *him* and *her* careful instructions.   [not "he" and "she"]
> He seems *considerate* of our needs.   [not "considerately"]

Basic Formula   Now you have the basic formula for a sentence: Subject-Verb-(and usually) Complement. A sentence that has only these three parts, and usually a modifier or two, is short and direct. In general, it has no punctuation marks other than the final end mark (period, question mark, or exclamation point), which indicates the sentence is finished. In technical and business writing many of your sentences will include no more than the basic formula and a modifier or two because you will be more interested in making your writing clear to your reader than in anything else.

Types of complements

NAME _____ SCORE _____

DIRECTIONS In the following sentences the subject is already underlined once; the verb, twice. You should underline the complement or complements of each sentence with three lines. In the blank write *object* or *objects* if the complement or complements show something or someone that the verb affects or acts upon. Write *subject complement* or *subject complements* if the complement or complements show something about the subject. This exercise illustrates the importance of using the right form of a complement in a sentence.

EXAMPLES

The counselor is she. _____*subject complement*_____

The student consults her. _____*object*_____

1. The student is nervous and shy. _____

2. He wants a summer job with the recreation de-

   partment. _____

3. The application form for the job frightens

   him. _____

4. The counselor helps him with his application. _____

5. She seems courteous and pleasant to the stu-

   dent. _____

6. Her manner gives him confidence. _____

7. Soon the student feels less insecure. _____

8. The counselor shows him similar applications

   with the spaces filled in. _____

9. He finds these sample applications helpful. _____

10. His own application blank no longer looks

    threatening. _____

11. With his counselor's help he can now fill it

    out with confidence.   _____

12. The counselor has shown him the way to deal

    with forms.   _____

13. Forms of any kind will not seem intimidating

    in the future.   _____

14. The student has found the counselor's help

    invaluable.   _____

15. Who helped you with your first job applica-

    tion?   _____

Recognizing subjects, verbs, and complements: Exercise 1–16
a review

NAME _____ SCORE _____

DIRECTIONS   In the following sentences underline the subject once, the verb twice, and the complement three times. Remember that one or more of the sentence parts may be compound.

EXAMPLES

The State Employment Service offers the unemployed information about

jobs in their area.

What information do you need?

1. The State Employment Service provides information about jobs, hiring standards, and wages.

2. The services of the agency are free.

3. The State Employment Service is a branch of the United States Employment Service of the Department of Labor.

4. Counselors at the Employment Service help teenagers, young adults, and older people.

5. The counselors use aptitude tests to indicate young people's interests and potential abilities.

6. Sometimes counselors suggest training programs to develop skills for certain jobs.

7. The primary objective of the Employment Service is placement of individuals in suitable positions.

8. What use have you made of the State Employment Service?

9. The Employment Service maintains a year-round program of assistance to youth.

10. The agency develops permanent and summer jobs for youths in the area.

11. One special program of the Employment Service provides placement services for graduating seniors and school dropouts.

12. This special service only certain state employment offices have.

13. Do you know about the Job Information Service?

14. It furnishes a daily computerized list of jobs available in the immediate area.

15. Applicants can also learn about jobs available in other areas of the country through Job Information Service.

1e A phrase or a clause, as well as an individual word, may function as the subject or the complement of a sentence.

You are already familiar with a group of words that may function as the verb of a sentence—the verb phrase (*will be putting*) and the verb with a particle (*put up with*). A word group may also function as the subject and/or the complement of a sentence.

SUBJECT	*Keeping a careful record of expenses* was a part of our job.
COMPLEMENT	We were required *to keep a log of our daily expenditures.*
SUBJECT AND COMPLEMENT	*Whoever examined our log* could find *what we had spent our money for each day.*

The main types of word groups that function as subjects and as complements are verbal phrases and noun clauses.

Verbal Phrases   A phrase is a series of related words (words grouped together) that lacks either a subject or a verb or both. The verbal phrase is the kind that most frequently functions as a subject and/or a complement of a sentence. The main part of the verbal phrase is the verbal itself—a word that shows action, occurrence, or a state of being as a verb does but that cannot function as the verb of a sentence (see page 19). You may remember from your study of verbs and verbals in **1b** that verbals usually end in *ing*, *ed*, *en*, or are preceded by *to*. The verbal, along with the other words in its phrase, can function as the subject or the complement of a sentence just as an individual noun or pronoun can.

NOUN	*Machines* have eliminated many jobs. [subject]
VERBAL PHRASE	*Using machines in the place of workers* has eliminated many jobs. [subject]
NOUN	Machinery has increased the *efficiency* of many jobs. [complement]
VERBAL PHRASE	Machinery helps *to increase the efficiency of many jobs.* [complement]

Noun Clauses   A clause is a series of related words (words grouped together) that has both a subject and a verb. One kind of clause, referred to as a main clause or as an independent clause, is a sentence. The other, called a subordinate clause or a dependent clause, functions as a subject, a complement, or a modifier in a sentence. The subordinate clause functioning as a subject or a complement is usually introduced by one of these words: *who, whom, whose, which, that, whoever, whomever, what, whether, how, why,* or *where.* These introductory words are called clause markers; they are printed in boldface in the following examples.

NOUN	An *applicant* must fill out an application. [subject]
NOUN CLAUSE	*Whoever wants a job* must fill out an application. [subject]
NOUN	Applicants' responses to the questions often show their *skills* in composition. [complement]
NOUN CLAUSE	Applicants' responses to the questions often show *whether they can write well or not.* [complement]

OR

Applicants' responses to the questions often show *how well they can write.*   [complement]

In **1f** you will see that verbal phrases and subordinate clauses may also function as modifiers in sentences. In fact, they are more commonly used as modifiers than as subjects or complements.

Recognizing phrases and clauses used as subjects and as complements

NAME _____ SCORE _____

DIRECTIONS   In the first of each of the following pairs of sentences, the complete subject is underlined once or the complete complement is underlined three times. In the second sentence of the pair, underline once the clause or phrase that functions as the subject, or underline three times the clause or phrase that functions as the complement. Then in the blank write the first and the last words of the phrase or clause that is functioning as a subject or a complement.

EXAMPLE

A knowledge of future growth is important when one plans a career.

Knowing future employment possibilities is important when one plans a

career.   *Knowing ... possibilities*

1. Some corporations will employ fewer people during the next decade.

Some corporations expect to employ fewer people during the next decade.

_____

2. An exact forecast for a specific occupation is difficult.

Forecasting exactly the employment opportunities for a specific occupation

is difficult.   _____

3. Changes in national policy affect future growth of certain areas of employment.

Changes in national policy affect what growth certain areas of employment

will èxperience.   _____

4. For example, the government might sponsor a new area of scientific

research.

For example, the government might decide to sponsor a new area of scientific

research.   _____

5. The new government-sponsored program would increase the demand for scientists and laboratory personnel.

   The government's sponsoring of a new program of research would increase the demand for scientists and laboratory personnel.

   _____

6. Any predictions about future employment are based on certain basic assumptions.

   Predicting future employment is based on certain basic assumptions.

   _____

7. One basic assumption concerns a peacetime economy.

   One basic assumption is that the country will not be involved in a major war. _____

8. The changes caused by a war no one could accurately predict.

   What would happen as a result of war no one could accurately predict.

   _____

9. The framework of our country's economy must also continue.

   That the framework of our economy will continue is also a basic assumption. _____

10. People's basic attitudes toward work, education, income, and leisure must remain unchanged.

    That people's attitudes toward work, education, income, and leisure will not change is another basic assumption.

    _____

1f Modifiers are words or word groups that expand the basic formula of a sentence.

A sentence made up only of the three main parts, or the basic formula, is always short and direct, but it frequently lacks the additions necessary to make it entirely clear, as the following sentence illustrates:

The applicant had qualifications.

Almost any reader would want to know what applicant and qualifications for what. The basic formula is not usually very satisfying then.

An addition to the basic formula functions as a modifier, a word or a group of words that adds a kind of qualification or description. A modifier makes the word it modifies more exact in meaning.

The applicant *from Calabash, Michigan,* had the *best* qualifications *for the job.*

The first addition (*from Calabash, Michigan*) makes the subject (*applicant*) more exact in meaning, while the second and third additions (*best* and *for the job*) make the complement (*qualifications*) more exact in meaning.

Additions to the basic formula may be words, phrases, or clauses. The process of expanding or adding to the basic formula is sometimes referred to as *sentence combining.* By using a word, a phrase, or a clause addition, the ideas in two or more sentences may be combined.

TWO SENTENCES	The report was poorly written. It was rejected by the manager.
WORD ADDITION	The *poorly written* report was rejected by the manager.
TWO SENTENCES	The report contained several noticeable errors in grammar and spelling. It obviously had not been proofread by the writer.
PHRASE ADDITION	*Containing several noticeable errors in grammar and spelling,* the report obviously had not been proofread by the writer.
THREE SENTENCES	The manager examined the first page of the report. He did not bother to read any further. The report did not represent careful work on the part of the writer.
CLAUSE ADDITIONS	*After the manager had examined the first page of the report,* he did not bother to read any further *because it did not represent careful work on the part of the writer.*

Word Additions   Nearly all sentences have one or more articles—*a, an,* or *the.* No one talks or writes much without using these simple modifiers. But in addition to *a, an,* and *the,* most sentences use one or more other words to modify the subject, the verb, the complement, or an addition to one of these parts.

A *large* increase in employment is expected in the field of landscape architecture. [*Large* modifies *increase.*]

The increase is *largely* due to the *continued* interest in *city* and *regional environmental* planning. [*Largely* modifies *due; continues* modifies *interest;* and *city, regional,* and *environmental* modify *planning.*]

53

Punctuation   Single-word additions, or modifiers, are punctuated only if they are placed in an unusual position in the sentence or if they modify the whole sentence.

> *Attractive,* the grounds for the building contribute to a happy work environment. [usual position: *the attractive grounds*]
>
> *Surprisingly,* no employee objects to the long walk through the trees to enter the building.   [*Surprisingly* modifies the whole sentence.]

Two modifiers in succession are often punctuated when there is no *and* between them though *and* is understood. Where no *and* would fit, no comma is used.

> The *large, well-landscaped* grounds surrounding the building make the work environment pleasant.   [You could say "large and well-landscaped grounds."]
>
> *Beautiful public* gardens are also nearby.   [You would not say "beautiful and public gardens"; *beautiful* modifies *public gardens*, not just *gardens.*]
>
> *Both large* and *small* plants line the street curving up to the building.   [You would not say "both and large plants."]

Using word modifiers

Exercise 1–18

NAME _____ SCORE _____

DIRECTIONS   In each blank write a modifier that fits smoothly into the sentence. After each sentence explain the punctuation or lack of punctuation for each modifier added.

EXAMPLE

*Exhausted*_____, the boy collapsed into a chair in the living room.

Reason: *Modifier is out of its usual position—"the exhausted boy."*

1. The _____, _____ first day on the job was ended.   Reason:

2. _____, he looked forward to the next day.   Reason:

3. The work, _____ and _____, was neverthe-less interesting.   Reason:

4. And this _____ day had shown him a great deal about him-self.   Reason:

5. He was not a _____, _____ person.

Reason:

6. And his body, _____ and _____, proved his lack of conditioning.   Reason:

7. _____, he needed to begin a daily exercise program.

Reason:

8. His body would require _____ hours of sleep each night.

Reason:

9. He also _____ needed to eat a _____ break-fast each morning.   Reason:

10. _____, he would have to buy a pair of _____ shoes.   Reason:

Phrase Additions There are three types of phrase additions: appositives, prepositional phrases, and verbal phrases.

Appositives An appositive is a word or phrase that identifies or explains in some way the noun or pronoun it is placed next to. Usually the appositive follows the noun or pronoun it identifies or explains. Appositives are set off by commas—or sometimes by dashes or colons (see Section **17**)—except on the few occasions when they are needed to restrict the meaning of the noun or pronoun they refer to (see **12d**).

> *Working, a book by Studs Terkel*, was on the New York Times best-seller list, for many weeks. [The appositive explains what *Working* is.]
> I, *your teacher*, urge you to read *Working* before you choose your career. [The appositive explains who I is.]

The appositive addition allows the writer to combine the ideas that would otherwise be stated in two sentences.

TWO SENTENCES *Working* is a book by Studs Terkel. It was on the best-seller list for many weeks.

APPOSITIVE ADDITION *Working, a book by Studs Terkel*, was on the best-seller list for many weeks.

Prepositional Phrases The prepositional phrase is the most frequent type of phrase modifier added to the sentence. It begins with a preposition—a word like *in*, *on*, *between*, or *to*—and ends with a noun, an *ing* verbal, or a pronoun; *in* the middle, *on* the road, *between* the cars, *to* the right one, *without* our knowing.

A prepositional phrase used to modify one word within a sentence is usually not punctuated. But a prepositional phrase that modifies the entire sentence is almost always punctuated.

MODIFIER OF NOUN We examined the manual *of operation*.

MODIFIER OF VERB We studied the manual *for several minutes*.

MODIFIER OF SENTENCE We studied, *in fact*, every instruction and drawing carefully.

MODIFIER OF SENTENCE The illustrations, *in addition to the words*, are important in a

manual of operation.

Verbal Phrases A verbal phrase includes a verbal (see page 19) and the other words related to it—usually a modifier or modifiers and an object.

Applauding the speaker enthusiastically, the audience rose to their feet. [The verbal, *applauding*, is followed by an object, *speaker*, and a modifier, *enthusiastically*.]

To show their appreciation, the audience remained standing until the speaker had left the platform. [The verbal, *to show*, is followed by an object, *appreciation*, and a modifier, *their*.]

The verbal phrase addition allows the writer to combine the ideas that would otherwise be stated in two separate sentences.

TWO SENTENCES	The audience applauded the speaker enthusiastically. They rose to their feet.
VERBAL PHRASE ADDITION	*Applauding the speaker enthusiastically*, the audience rose to their feet.

Punctuation   Verbal phrases used as modifiers are usually punctuated by commas, whether they appear at the beginning, in the middle, or at the end of sentences.

BEGINNING	*Having limited herself to five main points*, the speaker finished her presentation in fifteen minutes.
MIDDLE	The speaker, *having limited herself to five main points*, finished her presentation in fifteen minutes.
END	The speaker finished her presentation in fifteen minutes, *having limited herself to five main points*.

Placement   Verbal phrases used as modifiers must be placed so that they clearly modify one word in the sentence, usually the subject. If the writer puts a verbal phrase in the wrong place or includes no word for the phrase to modify, the verbal phrase is called a dangling modifier (see also Section **25**). A dangling modifier is sometimes laughable and is always confusing.

DANGLING MODIFIER	*Having always enjoyed books*, the library was where Dean chose to work. [*Dean*, not the "library," enjoyed books.]
CLEAR MODIFIER	*Having always enjoyed books*, Dean chose to work in the library.
DANGLING MODIFIER	A great many titles and authors were learned last summer, *while picking up and shelving books*. [There is no word for the verbal phrase to modify.]
CLEAR MODIFIER	Dean learned a great many titles and authors last summer, *while picking up and shelving books*. [The verbal phrase now has a word to modify—*Dean*.]

Using appositives   Exercise 1-19

NAME _____ SCORE _____

DIRECTIONS   Combine each of the following pairs of sentences by making one into an appositive addition to the other. Place the appositive next to the noun it identifies or explains, and punctuate the appositive with commas.

EXAMPLE
The nurse practitioner is a relative newcomer to the field of the health sciences. The nurse practitioner can relieve the physician of many duties.

The nurse practitioner, a relative newcomer to the field of the health sciences, can relieve the physician of many duties.

1. The nurse practitioner is usually a graduate of an advanced nursing program. The nurse practitioner is involved in both preventive medicine and treatment of minor or chronic disorders.

2. The nurse practitioner is an important aid to the physician. The nurse practitioner can give physical examinations, record medical histories, and order laboratory tests.

3. Rapport is necessary for a successful joint practice. Rapport is a smooth working relationship between the physician and the nurse practitioner.

4. The employment of nurse practitioners in Shimshon has allowed doctors to spend more time with their patients. Shimshon is a town near Jerusalem.

5. The Shimshon Center was one of the first medical centers to make extensive use of nurse practitioners. The center found that nurse practitioners could handle 67 percent of the center's patients without a physician's direct aid.

Using appositives

DIRECTIONS   The appositive often says as much as a longer construction does. Reduce the number of words in each of the following sentences by making the *who* or the *which* clause into an appositive. Below the sentence, write the appositive that results from your revision.

EXAMPLE

Of the many areas open in nursing, one of the newest is that of the nurse practitioner, ~~who is~~ a professional trained to perform many of the duties of a physician.

a professional trained to perform many of the duties of a physician

1. Nursing as a career has come a long way since the days of Florence Nightingale, who was the founder of modern nursing.

2. The Nightingale Home for Nurses, which was the school Florence Nightingale founded in London in 1860, trained many nurses from all parts of the world.

3. Boston General Hospital and Bellevue Hospital in New York, which were the first educational centers for nursing in the United States, began their training programs in 1873.

4. The American Nurses Association, Inc., which was the first professional organization of registered nurses, was founded in 1896.

5. During the nineteenth and twentieth centuries there have been many famous nurses, such as Clara Barton, who was the founder of the American Red Cross.

Using prepositional phrases

Exercise 1-20

NAME _____ SCORE _____

DIRECTIONS   Decide whether each italicized prepositional phrase in the following sentences is a modifier of a sentence part or a modifier of the entire sentence. Punctuate with commas those prepositional phrases that modify entire sentences. In the blanks write the italicized prepositional phrases and include the punctuation marks that you have added for those phrases that modify entire sentences.

EXAMPLES

Certain types *of occupations* are expected to have unusual growth in the next decade.

of occupations

Health occupations, *for example,* are expected to grow faster than most other areas of employment.

, for example,

1. Excellent opportunities *for employment* are expected for dental assistants.

2. *In fact* almost fifteen thousand annual openings are expected for dental assistants.

3. There are *besides full-time positions* good opportunities for part-time work.

4. The increasing use of dental hygienists *by dentists* makes the outlook for that profession good too.

5. The employment possibilities *for dental laboratory technicians* are excellent as a result of increasing demand for dentures.

6. Other types *of medical practitioners* will also be needed in increasing numbers during the coming decade. _____

7. There will be *without doubt* a continuing demand for physicians. _____

8. The need for physicians *especially in rural areas* is expected to increase greatly. _____

9. Chiropractic has an unusual growth potential *because of greater public acceptance* of the profession. _____

10. The growth *in the pet population* is expected to increase the employment opportunities for veterinarians. _____

Using verbal phrases

NAME _____ SCORE _____

DIRECTIONS   Each of the following sentences has a verbal phrase written after it. Rewrite the sentence with the verbal phrase used as a clear modifier. Be sure to include the punctuation needed. (Most verbal phrases may be included in more than one place in their sentences.)

EXAMPLE
The labor force is involved in two kinds of industries.   broken down simply

Broken down simply, the labor force is involved in two kinds of industries.

1. One kind of industry is involved with the production of goods.   expected to increase slowly during the coming decade

2. Industries that provide services are expected to increase more rapidly than those that provide goods.   employing more than one-half of all workers

3. Some industries produce both goods and services.   not so easily categorized

4. Service-producing industries include such divisions as trade, government, transportation, public utilities, finance, insurance, and real estate.   requiring more and more college graduates

5. Citizens of the United States demand more service industries than ever before.   to keep up their standard of living

6. Government at the state and local levels has shown the largest growth of all service-producing industries.   having increased by about 90 percent between 1960 and 1974

7. State and local government is expected to need more and more college-trained employees.   to meet the public's demand for education, health, and protective services

8. Employment at the federal level of government will not be so readily available during the coming decade.   increasing only 20 percent between 1960 and 1974

9. You can determine the service areas that hold the most promise for future employment.   after studying graphs that show projected rates of growth

10. Health services are expected to expand more rapidly than any others.   to satisfy the public's demand for more and better health care.

Subordinate Clauses In **1e** you studied one kind of subordinate clause—the noun clause, which can function as a subject or a complement in a sentence. As you may remember, a subordinate clause, unlike a main clause, cannot stand by itself as a sentence because of the clause marker that introduces it.

MAIN CLAUSE   People demand more and more health services.

SUBORDINATE CLAUSE   *because* people demand more and more health services

SUBORDINATE CLAUSE   people *who* demand more and more health services

A subordinate clause, then, can be made a main clause, or a sentence, by leaving out the clause marker (*because* and *who* in the examples above). Or it can be used as a sentence addition, thus combining the ideas in two sentences.

TWO SENTENCES   People are demanding more and more health services. There are excellent opportunities for employment in almost all health-related occupations.

SUBORDINATE CLAUSE *Because people are demanding more and more health services,*
ADDITION   there are excellent opportunities for employment in almost all health-related occupations.

TWO SENTENCES   People demand more and more health services. Not all of them are willing to pay for these services.

SUBORDINATE CLAUSE Not all people *who demand more and more health services* are
ADDITION   willing to pay for them.

Placement and Punctuation   Subordinate clauses that are introduced by clause markers like *because, since, although, if,* and *when* may be added to a sentence at various places. When such a subordinate clause is added in front of a main clause, it is followed by a comma; when it is added in the middle of a main clause, it is usually set off by commas (a comma at the beginning and end of the addition); when it is added after a main clause, it is usually unpunctuated.

BEGINNING   *When our country was first settled,* almost every worker was a farmer.

MIDDLE   Almost every worker, *when our country was first settled,* was a farmer.

END   Almost every worker was a farmer *when our country was first settled.*

In general, subordinate clauses introduced by clause markers like *which, that, who, whom,* and *whose* may be added to sentences only after the words they modify; otherwise, the clauses are misplaced modifiers.

MISPLACED MODIFIER In 1974 agriculture employed only about 4 percent of our nation's workers *which was once our major industry.*

CLEAR MODIFIER   In 1974 agriculture, *which was once our major industry,* employed only about 4 percent of our nation's workers.

A restrictive (defining) subordinate clause is not punctuated because it limits the meaning of the words it follows and is, consequently, essential to the meaning of the sentence. A nonrestrictive (nondefining) subordinate clause, on the other hand, is punctuated, usually with commas, because it is not essential to the meaning of the sentence. The clause marker *that* almost always introduces a restrictive (defining) subordinate clause.

RESTRICTIVE CLAUSE   The person *who decides to be a farmer* faces many hardships.   [The clause defines or identifies the kind of person who faces many hardships.]

NONRESTRICTIVE CLAUSE   My nearest neighbor, *who is a farmer,* faces many hardships.   [The word *neighbor* is identified or defined by the modifier *nearest.*]

RESTRICTIVE CLAUSE   My neighbor is not discouraged by the hardships *that he endures.*   [The word *that* introduces a restrictive clause.]

Main and subordinate clauses

NAME _____ SCORE _____

DIRECTIONS   Make each of the following subordinate clauses into a main clause by rewriting it without the clause marker. In the blank write the clause marker you have omitted.

EXAMPLE
some college graduates who are facing employment
    difficulties during the 1980s

*who*

Some college graduates are facing employment difficulties during the 1980s.

1. in the coming decade many college graduates who will take jobs for which they are not trained

    _____

2. certain areas, like clerical, service, and blue-collar occupations, that traditionally have been filled by employees without degrees

    _____

3. since many college graduates have already taken these jobs

    _____

4. the job market, which is highly mobile during the 1980s

    _____

5. college-trained people who will work at blue-collar jobs for only a short time   _____

6. because many employees will be dissatisfied with their occupations   _____

7. while the poor economic conditions of the 1970s may continue   _____

8. certain areas, like aerospace, that suffered severe cutbacks in the early 1970s   _____

9. many aerospace workers who were forced to seek alternative areas of employment   _____

10. when inflation forces many housewives to seek employment outside the home   _____

70

Using subordinate clauses

NAME _____ SCORE _____

DIRECTIONS   After each of the following main clauses (sentences) is a subordinate clause. Combine the subordinate clause with the main clause, using commas whenever necessary. If the subordinate clause may be added at more than one place, write a checkmark (✔) at the right.

EXAMPLES

c. College graduates will face stiff competition in most occupa-

tions. If present trends continue,   ✔

Many students train for their professions in two-year

colleges. who do not want a B.S. or B.A. degree   _____

1. The number of students entering junior and community col-

   leges is increasing rapidly, because these colleges can suc-

   cessfully train students for many occupations in two years or

   less   _____

2. The outlook for jobs during the 1980s varies according to the

   occupation. although there is a general shortage of openings

   for graduates of both four-year and two-year colleges   _____

3. A need for graduates in most engineering fields is expected. if

   past trends continue   _____

4. On the other hand, there is a surplus of graduates, who are

   trained in teaching and biological sciences   _____

5. Obviously, students must be increasingly aware of the job

market.   if they are to find suitable work after graduation   _____

6. Today's students must think of marketing their skills.   who

want jobs   _____

7. Careful planning must be a part of a student's education.

which considers the skills needed by the job market   _____

8. Thus students must choose their subjects carefully.   when

they are scheduling their classes for the semester or quarter   _____

9. Certain subjects, like composition and basic arithmetic, are

needed.   since the skills taught relate to success in most oc-

cupations   _____

10. In the 1980s there are jobs for all graduates.   who have trained

themselves for the openings available   _____

1g One main clause may be added to another main clause.

Sometimes a writer has two equally important ideas to set forth. The ideas are related, but one idea is not subordinate to the other. The writer may then write two main clauses and join them by a word like *and*, *but*, *or*, *nor*, or *for* or by a word or phrase like *however*, *therefore*, *then*, or *for example*. (See the Appendix for lists of joining words and phrases.) By far the most commonly used joining words are *and* and *but*. *And* suggests simply that an additional idea is coming, while *but* suggests that a contrasting idea is coming.

AND   Clerical occupations require a variety of skills, *and* they attract those who like to work with things as well as those who like to work with people.

BUT   The employment picture for some office occupations is good, *but* it is bad for those that are increasing their use of advanced office machinery.

HOWEVER   There is still a significant demand for record keeping in the 1980s; *however*, many of the filing jobs are being handled by computers.

If you overdo the joining of main clauses with *and*, your style will be childish. Save the *and*'s for ideas that should be stressed equally. Use a subordinate clause and main clause when one idea is dependent upon another. Or use two separate sentences when there is no strong relationship between the two ideas.

CHILDISH   I always wanted to be a secretary, and it was pleasant for me to think about writing letters and reports for an important business executive. I liked the idea of sitting behind a desk most of the day, and I enjoyed working with business machines. I thought I was cut out for the role of secretary, and I took a secretarial course at the community college in my area.

BETTER   I always wanted to be a secretary. It was pleasant for me to think about writing letters and reports for an important business executive. I liked the idea of sitting behind a desk most of the day, and I enjoyed working with business machines. Since I thought I was cut out for the role of secretary, I took a secretarial course at the community college in my area.

You will notice that the better paragraph has only one sentence in which two main clauses are joined by *and*, whereas the childish paragraph has three such sentences.

Punctuation Either a comma or a semicolon shows the reader that one main clause has ended and another is about to be added. The punctuation mark is written after the first main clause, just before the joining word. When two main clauses are joined by a word like *and* or *but*, a comma is used. When the two main clauses are joined by a word like *however* or a phrase like *for instance*, a semicolon is used. A comma is often added after a long joining word or a phrase—for example, after *however*, *on the other hand*, or *for example*. (Some writers use a comma after *therefore*; others do not.) And, finally, when two main clauses are joined by no word, a semicolon is used:

AND   The opportunities for receptionists are expected to increase during the late 1980s, and this occupation, unlike file clerking, should not be affected by automation.

HOWEVER   Thousands of job openings are expected for cashiers during the next few years; however, future growth may slow because of the widespread use of automated check-out systems.

NO JOINING WORD   Some clerical occupations depend on people more than on machinery; job openings in these areas will be increasing rapidly during the 1980s.

Combining main clauses

Exercise 1–24

NAME _____ SCORE _____

DIRECTIONS   Combine the second main clause with the first one, using a joining word like *and* or *however* or no joining word at all. Be sure to use either a comma or a semicolon at the end of the first main clause. In the blank write the joining word you have used and the punctuation included. If you used no joining word, simply list the punctuation mark included.

EXAMPLE

People who enjoy sales work can choose from a variety of occupations/ ; *for example,* + They can become insurance agents, real estate brokers, or retail trade salesworkers.

; for example, _____

1. There are thousands of openings in real estate sales each year. Many beginners have to transfer to other occupations because of the competitive nature of the occupation. _____

2. There should be eight hundred or more annual openings for models during the last half of the 1980s. The glamour of the occupation will attract many more than eight hundred applicants. _____

3. Self-service gasoline stations have eliminated the need for many attendants. There are still thousands of openings for service station attendants.

   _____

4. A few areas are expected to have a large number of openings for salespeople. The need for automobile parts salespeople is expected to increase greatly because of the growing number of motor vehicles.

   _____

5. Employment for route drivers is not expected to increase during the coming decade. Neither is employment for manufacturers' salesworkers.

   _____

6. Sales work is open to high-school as well as to college graduates. It is open to people who want to work for someone else as well as to those who want to run their own businesses.

   _____

Combining main clauses

7. Salesworkers must enjoy meeting people. Someone who is not at ease with strangers or who does not understand the needs of others should not enter sales work.   _____

8. Sales work probably requires more exceptional character traits than any other occupation. A good salesperson is imaginative, self-confident, ambitious, and energetic.   _____

9. Arithmetic skills are not required of all sales occupations. They are clearly an asset in any sales position.   _____

10. Many people in sales must be willing to travel. Some salespersons spend as much as four or five months of the year on the road.   _____

2

Write complete sentences.

A sentence fragment is usually a phrase (a group of related words that lacks either a subject or a verb or both) or a subordinate clause (a group of related words that has both a subject and a verb but that is introduced by a clause marker—a word like *who, which, that, if, since,* or *because*).

PHRASE	being asked to prepare a report for your employer
SUBORDINATE CLAUSE	when you are asked to prepare a report for your employer
SENTENCE	You are asked to prepare a report for your employer.

Few people write isolated fragments; rather they write fragments as parts of a paragraph. They needlessly separate what should be sentence additions from the main clauses they belong with. Notice that the writer of the following has mistakenly separated what should be sentence additions from the main clause they belong with.

> When you are asked to prepare a report for your employer. You may panic at the assignment. Realizing that your writing skills as well as your knowledge of your field will be examined carefully.

When the underlined words are treated as additions to the main clause, and are punctuated with commas, the fragments are avoided.

> When you are asked to prepare a report for your employer, you may panic at the assignment, realizing that your writing skills as well as your knowledge of your field will be examined carefully.

Of course, the fragments may also be avoided by making the underlined words into main clauses themselves, but the writing that results sounds childish.

> You are asked to prepare a report for your employer. You may panic at the assignment. You realize that your writing skills as well as your knowledge of your field will be examined carefully.

Usually, then, the best correction for a sentence fragment is to connect it with the main clause it has been carelessly separated from. The exercises in this section will provide you with experience in making fragments into additions to main clauses and in correctly punctuating these additions.

Avoiding phrase fragments   Exercise 2–1

NAME _____ SCORE _____

2a To avoid fragments, connect verbal phrases, prepositional phrases, and appositives to the independent clauses they belong with.

DIRECTIONS   Join the sentence fragment to the main or independent clause it has been separated from. Use a comma either before or after the fragment. (You will, of course, have to change the capitalization of one of the word groups.) In the blank write either *a* or *b* to show which of the word groups is the fragment.

EXAMPLES

ᵃAn important part of any job, ᵇ*t*The business report is usually

presented in written form.   *a*

ᵃMany reports are quite simple, ᵇ*r*Requiring no more than one

page of composition.   *b*

1. ᵃMost reports are deductive in format. ᵇThe main point of the

report being presented first and the supporting facts following. _____

2. ᵃUnlike business letters, which always follow a deductive ap-

proach. ᵇReports may sometimes have an inductive format.   _____

3. ᵃIn an inductive type of report. ᵇThe facts or supporting points

of proof are listed first.   _____

4. ᵃThen follows the main point or points of the report. ᵇOften a

conclusion or recommendation drawn from the facts

presented.   _____

5. ᵃUsually sent to the stockholders of the company or corpora-

tion. ᵇMost such long reports are written by professional

technical writers within the corporation or by outside con-

sulting firms.   _____

81

6. [a]Not so formal in style nor so complex to prepare. [b]Short reports are usually written by an ordinary office worker. _____

7. [a]To help an individual or a group of individuals make a deci-sion. [b]A short business report presents the facts needed to support a recommendation or a conclusion. _____

8. [a]Business reports help their readers make any number of deci-sions. [b]Such as the practical application of a procedure or the workability of a project. _____

9. [a]Often a permanent record to be kept on file. [b]A report may help a writer to prepare a future report of a similar nature. _____

10. [a]Before preparing any report. [b]The writer should be clear about the purpose of the report. _____

Avoiding subordinate clause fragments   Exercise 2-2

NAME _____ SCORE _____

2b To avoid fragments, connect subordinate clauses to the main clauses they belong with.

DIRECTIONS Join the subordinate clause to the main clause it has been separated from. Use a comma after the subordinate clause if it comes before the main clause; use no comma if the subordinate clause follows the main clause unless it is introduced by the clause marker *although*. (You will, of course, need to change the capitalization of one of the clauses.) In the blank write either *a* or *b* to show which word group is the fragment.

EXAMPLES

ᵃBefore a report is requested, ᵇᴵts probable usefulness to the

company should be considered.   *a*

ᵃUnnecessary reports should be eliminated, ᵇᴮecause they are

expensive and time-consuming to produce and distribute.   *b*

1. ᵃBecause routine reports are written frequently. ᵇPrepared

   forms are often used.   _____

2. ᵃIf a company receives frequent inquiries about its products. ᵇA

   prepared form providing the information requested saves both

   time and energy.   _____

3. ᵃPrepared forms are used in most medical fields. ᵇSince definite

   information must be presented.   _____

4. ᵃWhen patients report for dental or medical checkups. ᵇThey

   are usually asked to respond to a definite set of questions. _____

83

5. ªThe answers that patients supply may become the basis for longer, more formal reports. ᵇWhenever the dental or medical firm needs to supply patients with progress reports or insurance companies with detailed statements of claims. _____

6. ªWhereas formal reports often require a long time to prepare. ᵇShort routine reports can be handled in a matter of minutes. _____

7. ªWhile the forms of reports vary. ᵇNo report is useful unless the information included is accurate, objective, and carefully organized. _____

8. ªThe first job of the writer is to determine the audience for the report. ᵇBecause who is to read the report and what purpose it is to serve determine the type of report to be prepared. _____

9. ªIf similar reports have been completed in the past. ᵇThe writer should read them carefully before preparing the new report. _____

10. ªA past report will usually keep the writer from wasting a great deal of time. ᵇAlthough, unfortunately, previous reports are often unavailable because they have been lost in someone's files. _____

Avoiding subordinate clause fragments

NAME _____ SCORE _____

DIRECTIONS   Join the subordinate clause to the main clause it has been separated from. If the subordinate clause defines or limits in some way the meaning of the term it refers to, use no comma before it. If the subordinate clause simply adds useful information about the term, use a comma before the clause marker. No comma should be used before the clause marker *that*. (See **1f.**) (You will, of course, have to change the capitalization in each subordinate clause.) In the blank write the clause marker, if one is included, that signals the beginning of the subordinate clause fragment. (**Note:** Sometimes *that* is omitted when the subordinate clause is joined to the main clause.)

EXAMPLES

As employee of any business, you may receive a request for a report, That you are asked to prepare to certain specifications.

that

If the request comes to you in written form, carefully note the authorization, Which should make clear the exact nature of the report you are to prepare.

which

1. After underlining all the major points in the authorization, make a list of any questions. That you have about the nature of the report.

_____

2. If you do have questions, you may either call or write the person. Who requested the report.

_____

3. If you call the person, you may want to follow up the telephone conversation with a memorandum. That spells out the understandings you and the person have reached about the report.

_____

4. Let us assume that Mr. Brooks has written to you requesting a report. Which should list the new equipment and supplies needed by your office for the next financial year. _____

5. After reading the request carefully, you find that you have several questions about the exact information wanted by Mr. Brooks. Who is your immediate supervisor and also the manager of the company. _____

6. You first make a list of the questions. That you want Mr. Brooks to answer. _____

7. Perhaps your questions concern the meaning of "new" supplies and equipment and the amount of detail to be supplied about each item. That you plan to list. _____

8. You consult previous reports. Your predecessors have prepared. _____

9. Afterward you call Mr. Brooks. Who is happy to respond to any questions left unanswered by your reading of previous reports. _____

10. Your next problem is to collect the information. That you will need to prepare the report. _____

Avoiding other types of fragments

NAME _____ SCORE _____

2c To avoid fragments, connect the second part of a compound (two-part) verb or complement or a list of items to the main clause it belongs with.

DIRECTIONS   Join the second part of the compound verb or complement or the list of items to the main clause it belongs with. Use no comma before the second part of the compound verb or complement unless there is an addition to the main clause that must be set off. Use a comma or a colon before a list that you attach to the main clause: use a comma if the list is introduced by a phrase like *such as;* use a colon if there is no introductory phrase. (You will, of course, have to change the capitalization of each word group that you join to the main clause.) In the blank write *compound* if the fragment that you join to the main clause is the second part of the verb or complement; write *list* if the fragment is a list of items.

EXAMPLES

Sources of information for reports are either primary, which include data obtained firsthand/, ~~O~~r secondary, which include data obtained through gathering and assembling the research done by others.   *compound*

Information from primary sources is obtained in several ways: ~~B~~y questionnaires, by experiments, and by surveys.   *list*

1. Information from primary sources is obtained firsthand. And, consequently, has not been analyzed by someone else.   _____

2. Gathering information from primary sources is usually more time-consuming. And also more costly than consulting secondary sources.   _____

3. Thus, when writing a report, you should consult secondary sources first. And use them to avoid duplicating someone else's work. _____

4. Secondary sources are found in three places. Libraries, research departments in some companies, and, occasionally, data-gathering firms. _____

5. There are many kinds of libraries available. Such as school, college, and municipal. _____

6. Information may be recorded by summarizing from books or articles. Or by making notes on cards. _____

7. You may obtain information about office equipment and supplies from several primary sources. By studying manufacturers' brochures, by observing other offices, and by attending sales and professional conventions. _____

8. As you collect your information, you will need to organize your findings. And evaluate them. _____

9. If you do your research carefully, you may have more information than you need. Or more than your supervisor will care to read about. _____

10. Your last step before writing a report is to decide on a final plan for presentation. And to eliminate all the information that does not suit your plan. _____

Avoiding sentence fragments: a review

Exercise 2-5

NAME _____ SCORE _____

DIRECTIONS Each sentence or fragment in the following paragraphs is numbered. Circle the numbers of the ten fragments. Then connect the fragments to the main clauses they belong with. (In a few cases a fragment can be joined to either of two main clauses. Also, a few fragments occur in succession.) Change the capitalization and include commas and colons as needed.

¹Your final written report will probably fall into one of three categories. ²The memorandum, the letter, or the short informal report. ³The memorandum and letter forms are alike. ⁴Except that the letter is slightly more formal. ⁵And will probably be circulated outside the company. ⁶Most likely, though, the information you have gathered will be presented in the form of the short informal report. ⁷Which is usually no longer than ten pages. ⁸If your subject is limited to the acquisition of new office equipment and supplies. ⁹You should have little trouble with the final organization. ¹⁰The various kinds of equipment and supplies serving as the basis for your paragraphing.

¹¹Your report will probably be made up of several sections. ¹²The title page should be followed by the letter or memorandum requesting or authorizing the report. ¹³Or by a statement that such a report was requested or authorized and by whom. ¹⁴The body of the report itself should include a clear and concise statement of the purpose of the report. ¹⁵Next should come a summary of your findings. ¹⁶Including a description of the method or sources used to arrive at the find-

ings. [17] Such as surveys, questionnaires, direct observations, and research. [18] Finally, you should present your recommendations. [19] Which will include the list of supplies and equipment you feel should be purchased, together with information about the best products available, their particular features, and the prices of those products that you are recommending be purchased. [20] Headings should be used within the body of the report to make clear the three main divisions: purpose, findings, and recommendations.

3

Avoid comma splices and fused sentences.

In Section **1g** you learned that when one main clause is added to another, either a comma or a semicolon is the standard mark of punctuation between the main clauses. A comma is the mark used whenever the main clauses are connected by a coordinating conjunction: *and*, *but*, *or*, *nor*, *so*, *for*, or *yet*.*

> Most people think of a report as a written document, *but*, in reality, employees present almost as many oral reports as written ones.

If the coordinating conjunction is omitted, then the standard mark of punctuation between the main clauses becomes the semicolon, or sometimes the colon, if the second clause explains the first one.

> Most people think of a report as a written document; in reality, employees present almost as many oral reports as written ones.
>
> Employees may present oral reports to a variety of people: they may be called on for oral presentations by their immediate supervisors, by the upper management of their companies, and, on occasion, even by the general public.   [Here the second main clause does not present a related point but rather explains the idea of the first main clause.]

Even if the coordinating conjunction is replaced by another type of connecting word—a conjunctive adverb (*thus*, *then*, *therefore*, *however*) or a transitional expression (*on the other hand*, *in fact*, *for example*, *to sum up*)—the standard mark of punctuation between the main clauses is still the semicolon.

> Most people think of a report as a written document; *however*, in reality, employees present as many oral reports as written ones.

Note: Remember that a conjunctive adverb or a transitional expression may be used as an addition to a main clause rather than as a connector of main clauses. In this case, of course, the conjunctive adverb or transitional expression may be set off by commas: "Few employees, however, escape the task of writing some written reports each year."

To use a comma between main clauses not connected by a coordinating conjunction is to make a comma splice error; to use no punctuation mark at all is to write a fused sentence.

---

* Some writers consider *yet* a conjunctive adverb rather than a coordinating conjunction, so they use a semicolon rather than a comma preceding it when it connects two main clauses.

COMMA SPLICE Most people think of a report as a written document, in reality, employees present almost as many oral reports as written ones.

FUSED SENTENCE Most people think of a report as a written document in reality employees present almost as many oral reports as written ones.

In addition to the use of the semicolon, there are two other ways to correct a comma splice or fused sentence: write two separate sentences (if you want to emphasize both ideas), or make one of the main clauses into a subordinate clause (if you want to emphasize one idea more than the other).

TWO SENTENCES Most people think of a report as a written document. In reality, employees present almost as many oral reports as written ones. [Both ideas receive added emphasis by being presented in two short sentences.]

SUBORDINATION Although most people think of a report as a written document, in reality, employees present almost as many oral reports as written ones. [The idea in the second or main clause is emphasized.]

The exercises in this section will give you experience in correcting comma splices and fused sentences in all three ways: the use of the semicolon or colon, the use of two separate sentences, and the use of subordination.

Avoiding comma splices and fused sentences   Exercise 3-1

NAME _____ SCORE _____

3a Use a semicolon between two closely related main clauses not connected by a coordinator like *and* or *but*. (If the second main clause explains the first, use a colon.) Or rewrite the main clauses as separate sentences. Or make one of the clauses into a subordinate clause addition.

Note: Be especially careful to avoid comma splices and fused sentences in divided quotations: "Prepare an oral report as carefully as you would a written one," my technical writing instructor advised**.** (not **,**) "Be especially conscious of your audience in preparing an oral report."

DIRECTIONS   In the following fused and comma-spliced sentences, insert an inverted caret (**V**) Where two main clauses come together. Then correct the error in the way you think best. Write **;** in the blank if you use a semicolon to make the correction, **:** if you use a colon, **.** if you use two sentences, and *sub* if you make one of the clauses a subordinate clause addition.

EXAMPLE

According to one survey, preparation of oral reports takes up

25.4 percent of a worker's time⌄;preparation of written re-

ports occupies 24.5 percent.   _____;_____

1. Technicians write many descriptive reports⌄;they may also

   write one or more analytical reports each year.   _____;_____

2. A telephone technician working away from the plant usually

   submits a report on the work completed during a given shift,

   the report describes all breakdowns in telephone service and

   the steps taken to restore service.   _____

3. Technicians frequently write descriptive reports about changes

   in product specifications these reports are as essential to the

   company as the products themselves.   _____

93

4. Smaller companies depend on technicians to write most of the descriptive literature about their products technicians may also write the instructions that appear on labels. _____

5. The second major kind of report is the analytical one, it summarizes and evaluates tests performed by the company. _____

6. The computer has not eliminated analytical reports in small companies technicians tabulate and report test results. _____

7. "Whatever kind of report writing is to be done, certain skills are essential," my technical-writing instructor pointed out, "clarity, conciseness, and accurate word choice are the most important skills." _____

8. Supervisors are often shocked by the poor spelling of their employees many comment that their employees' spelling ranges from "poor" to "atrocious." _____

9. A report that has misspelled words in it is not well received the misspelled words cast doubt on the report's accuracy. _____

10. "Companies will not tolerate technicians who cannot spell correctly," one company president remarked, "if a technician misspells a common word in the description of a product, the customer does not trust the product." _____

Avoiding comma splices and fused sentences   Exercise 3–2

NAME _____ SCORE _____

3b   Use a semicolon between two main clauses joined by a word like *however* or *therefore* or a phrase like *for example* or *on the other hand*.

DIRECTIONS   In the following fused and comma-spliced sentences, insert an inverted caret (**V**) where the two main clauses come together. Then add a semicolon if no mark of punctuation is there; if a comma is there, cross it out and add a semicolon. In the blank write the semicolon and the word or phrase that follows it, as well as any punctuation that follows the word or phrase.

EXAMPLE

The memorandum is the shortest, most direct

form of business communication; therefore

it is the form most frequently used within

companies.   *; therefore*

1. In a memorandum the conclusion reached by

    the writer is put first thus a memorandum is

    deductive in its approach.   _____

2. The body of the memorandum briefly supplies

    details about the conclusion, then it offers fur-

    ther assistance or information.   _____

3. A memorandum is generally short in fact, it

    should seldom run more than two pages. _____

4. A memorandum is used primarily to supply in-

    formation therefore it does not have to present

    recommendations.   _____

5. Memorandums should be dated and should include headings for instance, *To*, *From*, and *Subject* (often expressed *Re*) usually introduce a memorandum. _____

6. Information can, of course, be communicated orally, however, a memorandum provides a lasting record. _____

7. A spoken message may be ignored or forgotten, on the other hand, a memorandum demands attention and can be referred to again. _____

8. A report in letter form often supplies the same information that a memorandum would however, since the tone of the letter-report is formal, it may be circulated outside the company. _____

9. A letter-report may omit some of the parts of the usual business letter for example, it may omit the inside address, the salutation, and the complimentary close. _____

10. For ease of reading, the letter-report usually has headings and subheadings in addition, it may include tables or other illustrations. _____

Avoiding comma splices and fused sentences: a review

Exercise 3-3

NAME _____ SCORE _____

DIRECTIONS   In the following paragraphs insert an inverted caret (**V**) where two main clauses are incorrectly joined. Then correct the fused and comma-spliced sentences by writing in semicolons or colons, by adding a period and a capital letter to make two separate sentences, or by rewriting one of the sentences as a subordinate clause addition.

[1] There are certain conventions of style to be observed in report writing. [2] First, and most important, a simple, straightforward presentation is essential, poetic words and roundabout phrasing have no place in reports. [3] The main purpose of a report is to communicate information clearly therefore anything that interferes with clarity should be avoided. [4] Sentences in memorandums and reports are usually much shorter and less complex in structure than are those in other types of writing again clarity, not variety, is the primary aim of a report writer.

[5] Report writing is also less personal, less subjective, than other types of writing. [6] Personal pronouns are generally avoided, especially the first person *I* or *we* the first person pronoun makes the report seem to be the opinion of the writer rather than a collection of objective information. [7] In most composition courses, one is advised to avoid the passive voice because it weakens style, however, in reports the passive voice is often recommended because it eliminates the need for personal pronouns. [8] Furthermore, subjective evaluations like *expensive* and *out-*

standing should be avoided, the reader, not the writer, should make such judgments based on the facts presented. [9] "This product is the most *exciting* thing our company has ever manufactured," one enthusiastic technician wrote, "it is a *must* for every household." [10] Needless to say, the supervisor reading the technician's report was not impressed with such subjective judgments rather, the supervisor was annoyed by the technician's failure to give an unbiased description of the product's operation.

[11] Finally, a report writer, like any other writer, must give credit for all facts and ideas gained through the research of others, otherwise, the writer is guilty of plagiarism, a serious offense in business and industry as well as in college. [12] Footnotes or source identifications, which are enclosed in parentheses within the body of the report, are necessary to show the help supplied by others in the preparation of the report then, of course, a bibliography is included at the end of the report or, in the case of a very long report, at the end of each chapter.

4

Use adjectives and adverbs correctly.

In Section **1f** you learned about the value of a modifier in making a word in the basic formula more exact in meaning.

> Writing a *good business* letter is *not* the *extraordinarily difficult* task *most* people feel that it is.

Without the modifiers—not to mention the articles—this sentence would not even have the same meaning, as is clearly shown when the sentence is written without any modifiers.

> Writing a letter is the task people think that it is.

The modifiers (*good*, *business*, and *most*) of the subjects (*letter* and *people*), the modifier (*not*) of the verb (*is*), the modifier (*difficult*) of the complement (*task*), and the modifier (*extraordinarily*) of another modifier (*difficult*) are all necessary to make the meaning of the sentence clear.

Adjectives   Modifiers of nouns and pronouns are called adjectives.

> Of all the types of *business* letters the *most difficult* one for *most* people to write is the
>
> letter of introduction.

Note: The pronouns *everyone* and *everybody* are modified by adverbs rather than adjectives because they are compound words made up of a pronoun (*one* and *body*) and an adjective (*every*): "*Almost* everyone can learn to write an effective business letter to a friend as well as to a stranger."

An adjective may also be used as the complement of a sentence, following a linking verb like *be*, *seem*, *feel*, or *look*.

> Business letters are not necessarily *dull* and *impersonal*.   [*Dull* and *impersonal* are predicate adjectives modifying the subject, *letters*.]

Adverbs   Modifiers of verbs and of other modifiers are called adverbs.

> A business letter to a friend or an acquaintance is *quite often highly* informal.   [*Often* modifies the verb *is; quite* modifies the adverb *often;* and *highly* modifies the adjective *informal.*]

When the modifier refers to a verb like *be*, *seem*, *feel*, or *look* rather than to the subject, an adverb, not an adjective, is used.

> The business executive looked *eagerly* through the pile of correspondence on his desk for a letter from his friend and business associate.

Form   Both adjectives and adverbs change their form when two or more things are being compared. An *er* on the end of a modifier or a *less* or *more* in front of it indicates that two things or groups of things are being compared (the comparative degree); an *est* on the end of a modifier or a *least* or *most* in front of it indicates that three things or groups of things are being compared (the superlative degree). Your dictionary shows the *er* and *est* ending for those adjectives and adverbs that form their comparative and superlative degrees in this way (for example—old, old*er*, old*est*). It also shows the changes for highly irregular modifiers (for example—good, *better*, *best*). If no form for the comparative or superlative is listed, then the adjective or adverb takes a *less* or *more* in front of it to form its comparative degree and a *least* or *most* to form its superlative degree (for example—difficult, *less* or *more* difficult, *least* or *most* difficult).

COMPARATIVE DEGREE   A business letter to a friend is no *more difficult* to write than a personal letter is.

SUPERLATIVE DEGREE   The *most difficult* letter to write is the one to a prospective employer.

Distinguishing between adjective and adverb modifiers   Exercise 4–1

NAME _____ SCORE _____

4a Use adjectives as subject complements and adverbs as modifiers of verbs, adjectives, and other adverbs.

DIRECTIONS   In each of the following sentences cross out the incorrect choice within parentheses and write in the blank the modifier that represents standard usage. To help you decide which is the correct choice, the word or words modified are underlined. (If you are uncertain about the part of speech of the underlined word or of the modifiers, consult your dictionary.)

EXAMPLE
(Almost, ~~Most~~) everyone must write many business

letters each year.   *almost*

1. Writing one's first business letter can (sure, surely)

   be a frustrating experience.   _____

2. Most people feel (reluctant, reluctantly) to write

   business letters.   _____

3. A business letter seems especially (difficult, diffi-

   cultly) if one waits too long before beginning it.   _____

4. Business letters should be written when one feels

   (fresh, freshly).   _____

5. Thus it is (preferable, preferably) to write business

   letters in the morning.   _____

6. Waiting until late afternoon to begin a letter makes

   the task (especial, especially) burdensome.   _____

101

7. Planning a time for correspondence and sticking to the schedule is a (real, really) <u>important</u> part of writing effective letters.   _____

8. All correspondence <u>must be answered</u> (prompt, promptly).   _____

9. Any unnecessary <u>delay</u> in answering an important letter can prove (disastrous, disastrously).   _____

10. You are judged by employers as well as by customers on how (quick, quickly) you <u>respond</u> to their requests.   _____

Using the comparative and superlative degrees

Exercise 4–2

NAME _____ SCORE _____

4b The comparative degree of modifiers (used when making a comparison of two things) is formed either by adding *er* to the modifier or putting *more* in front of it; the superlative degree (for making a comparison of three or more things) is formed by adding *est* to the modifier or by putting *most* in front if it. (See also **18d**.)

DIRECTIONS   In each of the following sentences cross out the incorrect form or forms of the modifier within parentheses and write the correct form in the blank. If you do not know how to form the comparative or superlative degree of the modifier, consult your dictionary.

EXAMPLE
Business letters are written (~~frequent~~ ~~lier~~, more frequently) than reports. _____*more frequently.*_____

1. Keeping up with correspondence has become one of the (importantest, most important) concerns of all businesses. _____

2. The business letter is the (commonest, most common) form of written communication. _____

3. Some people find it (easier, more easy) to answer correspondence by telephone than to dictate or write letters. _____

4. Certainly, the telephone has made communication (simpler, more simple). _____

5. But the telephone has not eliminated the use of business letters because the written word is (exacter, more exact) than the spoken word. _____

6. Written communication also endures (longer, more long) than spoken communication.   _____

7. One executive in my company writes the (clearest, most clear, most clearest) business letters I have seen.   _____

8. This executive regards clarity and conciseness as the two (more essential, essentialest, most essential) qualities of good business letters.   _____

9. The three (more important, most important) general purposes of business letters are to get the reader to react as wished, to give the reader information, and to build goodwill.   _____

10. Of course, business letters also serve (specificer, more specific) purposes than these.   _____

Mastering adjective and adverb modifiers: a review   Exercise 4–3

NAME _____ SCORE _____

DIRECTIONS   In each of the following sentences cross out the incorrect modifier within parentheses and write the correct modifier in the blank. Then underline the word or words modified. (If you are uncertain about the part of speech of the word or words you underline or about the proper form of the modifier, consult your dictionary.)

EXAMPLE
This letter is the most (~~careful~~, carefully)

<u>written</u> piece of correspondence I

have seen.   *carefully*

1. (Almost, Most) all business letters have the same format or plan.   _____

2. The opening of the letter should make clear the purpose or purposes of the letter (quick, quickly).   _____

3. The body of the letter then develops (fuller, more fully) what has been said in the opening.   _____

4. Finally, the closing emphasizes a point that the sender considers the (more, most) important one in the letter.   _____

5. The closing also says goodbye as (courteous, courteously) as possible.   _____

6. There is only one (noticeable, noticeably) exception to this general format, or plan.   _____

7. The so-called "bad-news letter" opens (different, differently).   _____

8. Bad news is (easier, more easier) to bear if the writer begins on a positive note.   _____

9. For example, instead of opening with "We refuse your request," begin (pleasanter, more pleasantly) with "We wish we could respond favorably to your request."

_____

10. In other words, the writer of the bad-news letter must be (real, really) careful to maintain the receiver's goodwill while regretting the inability to grant the request.

_____

5

Use the correct form of the pronoun to show its function.

As you learned in Section **1c,** the form that a noun or pronoun has indicates the way it works in a clause: as a subject or subject complement, as an object, or as a possessive. The form of the noun or pronoun, referred to as its case, may then be subjective, objective, or possessive. Nouns change their form for only one case—the possessive. (You study the ways to indicate this change in both Section **1c** and in Section **15.**)

Certain pronouns, though, change their form for each case, and you must be aware of the various forms if you want to indicate the function of these pronouns in clauses.

Subjective	Objective	Possessive
I	me	mine
we	us	our, ours
he, she	him, her	his, her, hers
they	them	their, theirs
who, whoever	whom, whomever	whose

Subjective Case   The subjective case is used for subjects and for subject complements.

> *She* answers all letters of complaint.
> The best writer in the firm is *he.*

Note: You may find it more comfortable to avoid using the pronoun as a complement: "*He* is the best writer in the firm."

Objective Case   The objective case is used for both direct and indirect objects, for objects of prepositions, and for both subjects and objects of infinitives.

> The customer wrote *me* about his problem with our product.   [direct object]
> He gave *me* his opinion about what should be done to improve the product.   [indirect object]
> He sent the unused portion of the product to *me.*   [object of preposition]
> He asked *me* to refund his money.   [subject of infinitive, *to refund*]
> He wanted to tell *me* about his difficulty in using the product.   [object of infinitive, *to tell*]

Possessive Case   The possessive case is generally used before a gerund. As you may remember from Section **1b**, a gerund is a verbal that ends in *ing.* But a participle also sometimes has an *ing* ending. The possessive case is used before a gerund, which acts as a noun, but not before a participle, which acts as an adjective.

GERUND   I got tired of *his* criticizing my company's product.   [*Criticizing* acts as a noun, the object of the preposition *of.*]

PARTICIPLE   I found *him* unreasoning in his attack on our product.   [*Unreasoning* acts as an adjective, modifying *him.*]

Case forms of pronouns

NAME _____ SCORE _____

5a The subjective case (*I, we, he, she, they, who, whoever*) is used for subjects and subject complements; the objective case (*me, us, him, her, them, whom, whomever*) is used for objects of verbs and verbals, for objects of prepositions, and for both subjects and objects of infinitives (for example, *to go, to be*); the possessive case (*my, our, his, her, their, whose*) is generally used to modify a gerund.

subjective   objective   objective
> *He* expected *us* to accompany *him*.

subjective   possessive   objective
> *He* read about *their* critizing a product in a letter to *us*.

subjective   possessive   possessive
> *We* regret *his* not being able to attend *your* meeting.

DIRECTIONS   In the following sentences cross out the incorrect case form or forms within parentheses and write the correct form in the blank. To help you decide which form is correct, the function of the correct choice is written in *italics* after the sentence. (It would be helpful to read your answers aloud several times after they have been checked to accustom your ear to the sound of correct case forms.)

EXAMPLE
The letters that come to (~~she~~, her) each day require immediate

attention.   *object of preposition*   *her*

1. No one except (she, her) is qualified to answer the letters. *object of preposition* _____

2. Only (she, her) knows the history of the product. *subject* _____

3. One customer told about (him, his) trying to make the product burn. *modifier of gerund* _____

4. She wrote (he, him) about the flammability studies that had been conducted on the product. *object of verb* _____

5. It was (she, her) who defended the product's safety record. *subject complement* _____

6. Her letter was convincing enough to make (he, him) withdraw his complaint.   *object of infinitive*   _____

7. It was necessary for (she, her) to follow up her first response with additional correspondence.   *object of preposition and subject of infinitive*   _____

8. Her letters were impressive to all of (we, us) who read them.   *object of preposition*   _____

9. After observing (she, her) for one day, we realized how much of an employee's time is spent in responding to letters.   *object of gerund*   _____

10. A course in business letter writing seems a necessity for someone like (she, her).   *object of preposition*   _____

Pronouns in compounds and as appositives   Exercise 5-2

NAME _____ SCORE _____

5b A pronoun has the same case form in a compound (two or more) or an appositive (renaming) construction as it would if it were used alone.

> Mel and *I* took courses under Mr. Brabstock and *her*.   [Compare with "*I* took courses under *her*."]
> *She*, the director of product information for a local firm, taught *us* students what we needed to know about business correspondence.   [Compare with "*She* taught *us* what we needed to know about business correspondence.]

DIRECTIONS   In the following sentences cross out the incorrect case form within parentheses and write the correct form in the blank. (To decide which case form is correct, say aloud each part of the compound construction separately or say aloud the pronoun without the appositive that follows it, as illustrated in the examples.)

EXAMPLES

(We, ~~Us~~) students took business writing. [*We took business writing.*]   *We* _____

The best writers in the class were (she and he, ~~her and him~~). [*The best writer in the class was she; the best writer in the class was he.*]   *she and he* _____

1. (We, Us) students spent hours writing business letters.   _____

2. The practice was very helpful to (we, us) students.   _____

3. Finally, the format of a business letter was clear to (the rest of the class and I, the rest of the class and me).   _____

4. When (we, us) students entered the business world, we were prepared to write well.

          _____

5. Both (Peggy and he, Peggy and him) knew how to write a courteous refusal letter.

          _____

6. Writing a sales letter to a prospective client was also easy for (Tim and she, Tim and her).

          _____

7. (She, as well as he; Her, as well as him,) had had experience receiving and responding to orders.

          _____

8. Furthermore, the business writing course taught (Tim and she, Tim and her) how to write resquests for information or assistance.

          _____

9. Finally, (Peggy and he, Peggy and him) were taught to write and answer a claim or a complaint letter.

          _____

10. The best writers the company hired were (she and he, her and him).

          _____

Pronouns in subordinate clauses and with *self* added   Exercise 5–3

NAME _____ SCORE _____

5c The case of a pronoun depends on its use in its own clause.

> I think I know *who* the best writers are.   [Although *who* begins the clause that is the object of *I know*, in its own clause *who* is the subject complement: the best writers are *who*.]

5d *Self* is added to a pronoun only when a reflexive or an intensive pronoun is needed.

> I *myself* will answer the letter.   [intensifies *I*]
> I wrote a letter to *myself*.   [reflects back to *I*]
> The supervisor asked us to respond directly to *him*.   [NOT *himself*]

Note: *Hisself, theirselves,* and *its self* are nonstandard forms of *himself, themselves,* and *itself.*

DIRECTIONS   In the following sentences cross out the incorrect case form or forms within parentheses and write the correct form in the blank.

EXAMPLE
He was the personnel director (who, ~~whom~~) every-

one thought gave the best presentation.   *who*

1. The students wanted to know (who, whom) they should write about job opportunities within the company.   _____

2. The personnel director said they should first write (him, himself) for information and for application blanks.   _____

3. The completed application (its self, itself) and the request for an interview would be forwarded to the appropriate department head.   _____

4. The students found (them, themselves, theirselves) confronted with the need to write a difficult kind of business letter.   _____

5. The students (who, whom) had learned business writing were obviously best prepared for job hunting. _____

6. It was their instructor in business English (who, whom), they remembered, had said that writing skills were important in acquiring a first job. _____

7. When they were told the number of people in the company (who, whom) might read their letters, they realized how much their writing would represent them. _____

8. The practice letters they had written in business English proved worthwhile to (them, themselves, theirselves). _____

9. They wanted (whoever, whomever) read their correspondence to think of them as literate. _____

10. They also wanted to show their knowledge of correct form in business writing to (whoever, whomever) might read their letters. _____

Mastering case: a review   Exercise 5–4

NAME _____ SCORE _____

DIRECTIONS   In the following sentences cross out the incorrect case form or forms within parentheses and write the correct form in the blank. Determine the use of the pronoun in its own clause before you choose the case form.

EXAMPLE

The personnel director is the employee within the

company (who, ~~whom~~) usually answers letters

from job applicants.   *who*

1. Most companies send form letters to (whoever, whomever) they would like to interview for a job.   _____

2. The personnel director sends replies to the applicants that tell (they, them, themselves) briefly what they need to know about the interview: whom they are to see, at what time, on what day, where the interview is to take place, and what positions they are being considered for.   _____

3. It is important, of course, that the applicant understand (who, whom) he or she is to be interviewed by.   _____

4. The applicant should also be told what (she or he, her or him) should bring to the interview.   _____

5. Finally, the letter should explain the nature of any tests that will be given to (she or he, her or him) at the time of the interview.   _____

6. (Everyone, Everyone's) knowing what to expect will help the interview to progress smoothly and quickly.   _____

7. Applicants (who, whom) the company does not wish to interview should be politely informed of their rejection.   _____

115

8. A letter of rejection first thanks the applicant for the interest shown in the company and then explains that there is no immediate opening for (she or he, her or him). _____

9. Letters to highly qualified applicants may give additional information; for example, such a letter might begin, "(We, Us) at IBM felt that your qualifications are much better than our opening demands. Have you considered applying for a different position?" _____

10. A letter rejecting an application for a position or a request for an interview should, like any other bad-news letter, try to retain the goodwill of the applicant (who, whom) is being refused. _____

6

Master agreement of subject and verb and pronoun and antecedent.

In Sections **1b** and **1c** you learned about the importance of matching up the right subject and verb so that the two agree in number. Subjects and verbs must have the same number; a singular subject requires a singular verb, and a plural subject requires a plural verb. (Remember that an *s* ending shows plural number for the subject but singular number for the verb.)

SINGULAR   A good business <u>letter</u> <u>makes</u> clear the response that is expected from the recipient of the letter.

PLURAL   Good business <u>letters</u> <u>make</u> clear the responses that are expected from the recipients of the letters.

In the same way, a pronoun agrees in number with its antecedent, the noun that it replaces or refers to.

SINGULAR   A good business letter makes clear the *response that* is expected from the recipient of the letter. [Notice that the verb *is expected* is singular because the antecedent of *that*, *response*, is singular.]

PLURAL   Good business letters make clear the *responses that* are expected from the recipients of the letters. [Notice that the verb *are expected* is plural because the antecedent of *that*, *responses*, is plural.]

Mastering agreement requires that you be able to do three things: (1) match up the simple subject or subjects with the verb or verbs; (2) know which nouns and pronouns are traditionally singular and which are traditionally plural; and (3) identify the antecedent of a pronoun, the noun it refers to, so that you can determine the number of the antecedent.

Simple Subjects   To make the subject and verb agree in number, you must be able to recognize the simple subject of a sentence as well as the verb. You may remember from your study of Section **1c** that the simple subject is often surrounded by other words that are a part of the complete subject and that can easily be mistaken for the exact word or words that should agree in number with the verb.

117

SINGULAR A <u>device</u> that encourages quick responses from recipients of request letters <u>is</u> the stamped, addressed return envelope.   [The complete subject contains several plural nouns—*responses*, *recipients*, and *letters*—that must not be mistaken for the simple subject, which is singular.]

PLURAL <u>Devices</u> that encourage a quick response from the recipient of a request letter <u>include</u> the stamped, addressed return envelope, a reply card with answers to check, and free prizes or other rewards for a prompt response.   [The complete subject contains several singular nouns—*response*, *recipient*, and *letter*—that must not be mistaken for the simple subject, which is plural.]

Singular and Plural Nouns and Pronouns   Some nouns and pronouns are traditionally considered either singular or plural in number. For example, *the number* is always treated as singular whereas *a number* is treated as plural.

SINGULAR <u>The number</u> of request letters my company sends out each day <u>is</u> astoundings.

PLURAL <u>A number</u> of these requests <u>are</u> never <u>answered</u>.

Pronouns like *each*, *everyone*, and *someone* are traditionally singular, while pronouns like *both*, *some*, and *many* are traditionally plural.

SINGULAR <u>Each</u> of the letters we send out <u>is</u> direct but courteous.

PLURAL <u>Some</u> of the letters <u>request</u> payment of delinquent accounts.

Still other nouns and pronouns are sometimes singular in number and sometimes plural depending on their contexts in their sentences.

SINGULAR A <u>group</u> of request letters <u>has been examined</u> by management.   [Here *group* is considered a unit.]

PLURAL A <u>group</u> of employees <u>are taking</u> various business writing courses offered by their company.   [Here *group* refers to many individuals, not to a unit.]

Antecedents of Pronouns   In Section **1c** you learned that a pronoun takes its meaning from the noun it replaces. In addition, the pronoun takes its number from the noun it replaces or refers to—that is, from its antecedent.

SINGULAR   A *request that* is clearly stated is usually answered.   [*Request*, the antecedent of *that*, is singular in number; therefore *that* is also singular.]

PLURAL   *Requests that* are clearly stated are usually answered.   [*Requests*, the antecedent of *that*, is plural; therefore *that* is also plural.]

SINGULAR   *Each* of the one hundred women selected for the surveys sent us *her* response promptly.

PLURAL   *Most* of the women responded that *their* experience with our product had been good.

Note: Today most writers, and especially business writers, are making every effort to avoid sexism in the use of personal pronouns. Whereas writers once wrote, "*Each* of us should do *his* best," they now try to avoid using the masculine pronoun to refer to both men and women. To avoid sexism, some writers give both masculine and feminine pronoun references.

> Each of us did *his or her* best.
> Each of us did *his/her* best.

Other writers prefer to use *one's* in the place of *his or her*.

> One should do *one's* best.

Perhaps the easiest way to avoid sexism is to use plural pronouns and antecedents unless a feminine or a masculine pronoun is clearly called for, as *his* would be in reference to a male employee or *her* in reference to a female employee.

> All of *them* did *their* best.
> All of *us* did *our* best.

Subject and verb agreement

Exercise 6-1

NAME _____ SCORE _____

6a The verb agrees with its subject. (See also 1a).

A letter arrives from a competitor.

Letters arrive from competitors.

Be especially careful to have the verb agree in number with its subject when

(1) the subject or the verb ends in k or t:

Scientists study the results.

The manager asks for daily progress reports.

(2) the subject is followed by a prepositional phrase or a subordinate clause:

The purpose *of the reports* is clear.

The purpose, which was stated in all the reports, is clear.

(3) the subject follows the verb:

There are many daily reports from agencies of the government.

(4) the subject and subject complement do not have the same number.

(Usually you should rewrite the sentence, without using a form of *be*, to avoid the conflict in number.)

AWKWARD   Reports are one way to monitor progress within a company.

BETTER   Reports serve as one monitor of progress within a company.

DIRECTIONS   In each of the following sentences underline the subject with one line (remember that a verbal may act as a subject); then match it with one of the verbs in the parentheses. Cross out the verb that does not agree with the subject, and write in the blank the verb that does agree. (When all of your answers have been checked, read aloud each sentence, emphasizing the subject and verb.)

EXAMPLE

The purpose of persuasive letters (is, ~~are~~) to sell a

product, an idea, or a service.   *is*

1. Students (writes, write) persuasive essays in freshman

composition.   _____

2. The persuasive essay (attempts, attempt) to convince the reader that an opinion is correct.   _____

3. Persuasive essays usually (makes, make) use of emotional appeals.   _____

4. A persuasive letter, like a persuasive essay, (uses, use) emotional appeals.   _____

5. The writer's tactics (is, are) not obvious.   _____

6. An exaggerated emotional appeal sometimes (loses, lose) the reader's interest in the writer's message.   _____

7. There (is, are) several ways to begin a persuasive letter.   _____

8. The writer of persuasive letters (has, have) to remember that such mail may be uninvited.   _____

9. Included in the writer's duties (is, are) gaining the interest of the reader.   _____

10. A letter that fails to gain the reader's interest (is, are) promptly thrown into the wastebasket.   _____

Subject and verb agreement   Exercise 6–2

NAME _____ SCORE _____

DIRECTIONS   Rewrite the following sentences, replacing the plural subjects and verbs with singular ones and the singular subjects and verbs with plural ones. Underline the subject with one line, the verb with two lines. You will also have to change the articles (*a*, *an*, and *the*) to make the sentences sound right.

EXAMPLES
Persuasive letters usually arrive uninvited.

A persuasive letter usually arrives uninvited.

The reader has not requested such a letter.

Readers have not requested such a letter.

1. The writer of persuasive letters convinces readers to look beyond the first few lines.

2. The opening lines of a persuasive letter are extremely important.

3. There is a definite way to gain the readers' attention.

4. The opening of persuasive letters appeals to the readers' self-interest.

5. The opening promises certain rewards to the readers, like health, popularity, success, or some other personal benefit.

6. A successful advertisement suggests effective ways to open a persuasive letter.

7. The headlines of advertisements serve much the same purpose as the opening sentence of a persuasive letter.

8. The headline gets the audience to pay attention to the rest of the advertisement.

9. The benefit promised the audience is specific in successful advertisements and in persuasive letters.

10. The reward offered by Dale Carnegie's *How to Win Friends and Influence People* is clearly stated.

Singular and plural noun subjects   Exercise 6–3

NAME _____ SCORE _____

6b Some noun subjects are traditionally singular, while others are traditionally plural.

Those subjects that are traditionally singular include

(1) singular subjects joined by *or* and *nor* and subjects introduced by *many a:*

Neither the letter *nor* the advertisement has gotten results.

Many a letter goes unnoticed.

(2) collective nouns regarded as a unit:

The number of persuasive letters is amazing.

The *jury* has reached its decision.

(3) nouns that are plural in form but singular in meaning:

The news is depressing today.

Two thousand dollars is the cost.

(4) titles of works or words referred to as words:

"*Good Times*" is showing on television.

Those subjects that are traditionally plural include

(5) subjects joined by *and:*

A memo *and* a report have many similarities.

(6) a plural subject following *or* or *nor:*

Neither the manager *nor* his employees neglect correspondence.   [The verb agrees with *employees*, the part of the subject it is nearer to.]

(7) collective nouns that do not act as a unit:

A *number* of reasons are given for the company's success.

The staff are having difficulties agreeing.

DIRECTIONS   In each of the following sentences underline the subject (or subjects, if compound) with one line and match it (or them) with one of the verbs in the parentheses. Circle any key word or words that affect the number of the subject. Then cross out the verb that does not agree with the subject and write in the blank the verb that does agree.

EXAMPLE

(A)number of appeals (~~is~~, are) available to the per-

suasive writer.   _are_

1. Either health or comfort (is, are) a good choice.   _____

2. News about ways to improve status also (makes, make) a successful opening for a persuasive letter.   _____

3. Education and popularity (is, are) two other appeals.   _____

4. Either a promise of something good or ways to avoid unpleasant situations favorably (impresses, impress) most readers.   _____

5. "Do you make these mistakes in etiquette?" (is, are) one familiar opening.   _____

6. *These*, of course, (is, are) the key word; the reward promised by the advertisement must be exact.   _____

7. A number of other tactics (is, are) used to gain the reader's attention.   _____

8. New information and satisfaction of curiosity (is, are) frequently promised by persuasive letters.   _____

9. "Revolutionary!" or "Completely new!" (arouses, arouse) the reader's curiosity.   _____

10. The number of attention-getting words typically used as openers (is, are) surprisingly small.   _____

Singular and plural pronoun subjects

NAME _____ SCORE _____

6c Some pronoun subjects require singular verbs and references, while others require plural verbs and references.

(1) Pronouns like *each, one, anybody, everybody, everyone, either,* and *neither* are considered singular.

Everyone is ready to present a report.

(2) Pronouns like *both, many, several,* and *few* are considered plural.

Many have done *their* best.

(3) Pronouns like *all, any, half, most, none,* and *some* may be singular or plural, depending on the context (that is, depending on the rest of the sentence or paragraph, but they are more often considered plural than singular).

All have dedicated *themselves* to the project.

All of their dedication has been rewarded.

(4) A collective noun, like *staff* or *committee,* may require a singular or plural pronoun reference, depending on whether it is regarded as a unit. (See also 6b [2 and 7].) Usually, however, the noun is considered singular. When a plural sense is intended, a plural word, like *members,* is often used as the subject.

The *committee* has completed *its* report.

The members of the department are unhappy with the policy.

(5) The number of a relative pronoun (*who, whom, which, that*) used as a subject is determined by the number of its antecedent, the word it refers to.

This is the only *one* of the techniques that appeals to the reader.

This is one of the many *techniques* that appeal to readers.

DIRECTIONS   In the following sentences cross out the verb or pronoun in parentheses that does not agree with its subject or antecedent. Then enter the correct pronoun or verb in the blank.

EXAMPLE
One must quickly involve (one's, ~~their~~) reader in a

letter intended to persuade.   *one's*

1. Most of us (wants, want) to receive the benefits promised by the opening line of a persuasive letter. _____

2. Few of us (reads, read) far if we do not see the value of the product or service for ourselves. _____

3. One who (writes, write) successful persuasive letters will generally introduce the word *you* in the first few sentences. _____

4. The use of *you* helps readers to see (himself or herself, themselves) receiving the benefits of the product, service, or action. _____

5. "Is this the day you do something about your weight?" is an opening line that immediately (puts, put) us into the picture. _____

6. Since most of us (is, are) at least a little overweight, we are sure to read further. _____

7. Then follows a chart that (shows, show) desirable weights for men and women. _____

8. Almost everyone (checks, check) to see how his or her weight compares with the ideal weight. _____

9. Neither the male nor the female reader (wants, want) to be overweight in today's weight-conscious society. _____

10. Finally, then, the writer shows that the product advertised will reduce (one's, their) weight to the ideal level shown on the chart. _____

Mastering agreement: a review

NAME _____ SCORE _____

DIRECTIONS   In the following sentences cross out the verb or pronoun in parentheses that does not agree with its subject or antecedent. Then enter the correct pronoun or verb in the blank.

EXAMPLE
Most successful advertisements (~~appeals~~, appeal) to both our minds and our emotions.   *appeal*

1. Details (convinces, convince) our minds to buy what our hearts desire.   _____

2. Everyone (tries, try) to rationalize his or her desires.   _____

3. The details presented in the persuasive letter (provides, provide) the needed rationalization.   _____

4. If a person (wants, want) to buy a new car, he or she must be convinced that the car is really necessary.   _____

5. The characteristics of the car (gives, give) the reader proof that that particular car is needed.   _____

6. Other kinds of persuasive information (includes, include) a physical description of the product, the reputation of the company, and the test and performance data.   _____

7. Another source of persuasion (is, are) the testimonial of a satisfied customer.   _____

8. The famous ads of the past for the Charles Atlas body-building program (demonstrates, demonstrate) still another strategy: showing the reward in action.   _____

9. Many a young man bought the Charles Atlas body-building program hoping to see (himself, themselves) transformed into a powerful he-man like the one shown in the advertisement.   _____

129

10. Today, of course, one must be sure that the claims (one makes, they make) are true. _____

11. But there (is, are) usually many legitimate claims that can be made about a product or service if one knows the facts. _____

12. As a persuasive writer, you must emphasize the facts that (gives, give) your product an edge over your competitor's. _____

13. A successful persuasive letter usually (asks, ask) the reader to do something. _____

14. The closing of the letter (suggests, suggest) that the reader send for more information or fill out a questionnaire or an application form. _____

15. Writers of persuasive letters must make clear exactly what action (he expects, they expect) from the reader. _____

16. Most persuasive letters (follows, follow) a set formula: they arouse their readers' attention; they interest their readers in their product or service; they call for some response from their readers. _____

17. Sentences and paragraphs in a persuasive letter (is, are) short; the vocabulary is simple but mature. _____

18. The company or firm the writer represents must never seem to be talking down to (its, their) potential clients. _____

19. Neither sarcasm nor a condescending tone (is, are) appropriate. _____

20. As in any other kind of business letter, one of the main purposes of a persuasive letter (is, are) to build goodwill for the company or business. _____

7

Master verb forms.

7a Learn the main tenses of verbs.

Regular Verbs Most verbs are called regular verbs; that is, the changes they undergo to show tense or time are predictable: *ed* is added to the end of the present tense to form the past tense and the past participle, and *ing* is added to form the present participle. (See also **1b**.) From these four main parts of the verb—present, past, past participle, and present participle—together with helping verbs, like *is*, *has*, and *had*, all the tenses of verbs are formed.

PRESENT	I type the report.
PAST	I typed the report yesterday.
FUTURE	I will type the report tomorrow.
PRESENT PERFECT	I have typed the report many times.
PAST PERFECT	I had typed the report before the manager requested it.
FUTURE PERFECT	I will have typed the report before the manager requests it.
PROGRESSIVE	I am (was, will be, have been, had been, OR will have been) typing the report.

You may have noticed that other words in the sentence besides the main verb and its helping verbs express time—for example, *yesterday*, *tomorrow*, and *before*.

The future is frequently expressed by a form of the present tense plus a word like *tomorrow* and/or an infinitive.

I *am typing* the report *tomorrow*.
I *am going to type* the report *tomorrow*.

The present perfect tense is formed from the past participle and the helping verbs *has* and *have*. This tense suggests that an action was begun in the past but has been continued into the present.

She has typed the report carefully many times before.

They have typed the report carefully many times before.

The past perfect tense is formed from the past participle and the helping verb *had*. This tense suggests that an action was begun and completed before some time in the past.

He had typed the report a week before it was due in the manager's office.

The progressive form may be used for any of the regular tenses—present, past, future, present perfect, past perfect, and future perfect. It is formed from the present participle of the verb—the *ing* form—plus the helping verbs that are normally used for the various tenses. The progressive form of a verb suggests a continuing process.

He is typing the report.

He was typing the report when the manager came in.

He will be typing the report when the manager comes in.

Irregular Verbs   Irregular verbs do not form the past and past participle in the usual way; instead, they undergo various kinds of changes or, in a few cases, no change at all. (See the chart of frequently used irregular verbs in the Appendix.)

run, ran, run, running
choose, chose, chosen, choosing
burst, burst, burst, bursting

The dictionary lists all four parts of irregular verbs, usually at the beginning of the entry. The dictionary also lists all forms of regular verbs that undergo a change in spelling for the past, the past participle, or the present participle. This change in spelling is most frequently the substitution of *i* for *y*, the doubling of the last letter, or changing *y* to *id*.

try, tr*ied*, tr*ied*, trying
occur, occur*red*, occur*red*, occur*ring*
pay, pa*id*, pa*id*, paying

Did   When the helping verb *did* is used with a main verb, the writer emphasizes past time, but the main verb is in the present form. The *did* form of the past is used mainly for questions, for the negative, and for special emphasis.

Did she type the report carefully?

She did not (OR *didn't*) type the report carefully.

She did type the report carefully.

Do   The helping verb *do* (OR *does*) is also used for questions, for the negative, and for special emphasis.

Does she type reports carefully?

She does not (OR *doesn't*) type reports carefully.

She does type reports carefully.

Used   The helping verb *used* followed by an infinitive (*to* plus a verb) can be used to mean "was in the habit of" or "was accustomed to."

She used to type reports carefully.

7b Learn the uses of the passive voice.

In most sentences, the verb is in the active voice; that is, the verb expresses an action committed by the subject. But sometimes this pattern is reversed and the subject does not act but is acted upon; in this case the verb is in the passive voice. The passive voice is formed by placing a form of *be* in front of the past participle form of the verb (for example—*is typed, was typed, has been typed, will be typed*).

ACTIVE VOICE   The secretary carefully types reports.

PASSIVE VOICE   Reports are carefully typed by the secretary.

PASSIVE VOICE   The reports are then proofread several times.

As you probably noticed from the above examples, the object of a sentence with an active verb can become the subject of a sentence with a passive verb. The actual doer of the action of the passive verb is sometimes expressed after the preposition *by* (as in the first example of the passive voice) and is sometimes left unstated (as in the second example of the passive voice).

The passive voice is used when you do not know the doer of the action ("Mr. McDowell's store was robbed last night") or when you want to emphasize the verb or the receiver of the action of the verb ("A report is sometimes rewritten three times before it is submitted to upper management"). The passive voice, except in report writing, is sparingly used because it sounds highly impersonal and sometimes deprives writing of emphasis (see also Section **29**).

Regular and irregular verbs

NAME _____ SCORE _____

DIRECTIONS   Mastering verb forms, especially irregular verb forms, requires memorizing them (just as you would memorize multiplication tables or chemical formulas) and accustoming your ear to the correct forms. The best way to learn verb forms, then, is through written and oral drill of the five tenses of those verbs that cause difficulties; the five tenses are present, past, present or past perfect (both formed from the past participle), progressive, and the *did* form of the past.

Following the models given for the example, make up your own short sentences for the verbs listed. Use either *he* or *she* for your subject. (See your dictionary if you are unsure of the way to form any of the tenses.)

After you have written the sentences and your verbs have been checked, read the sentences aloud, emphasizing the verbs. If you stumble over a verb or if a verb form sounds strange to you, then you have probably discovered one that gives you trouble in speaking and writing.

EXAMPLE
draw

PRESENT
She draws an illustration.

PAST
She drew an illustration.

PRESENT PERFECT
She has drawn an illustration.

PROGRESSIVE PRESENT
She is drawing an illustration.

did FORM OF PAST AS A QUESTION
Did she draw an illustration?

1. suspect

PRESENT

PAST

PRESENT PERFECT

PROGRESSIVE PRESENT

did FORM OF PAST AS A QUESTION

2. begin

    PRESENT

    PAST

    PRESENT PERFECT

    PROGRESSIVE PRESENT

    did FORM OF PAST AS A QUESTION

3. blow

    PRESENT

    PAST

    PRESENT PERFECT

    PROGRESSIVE PRESENT

    did FORM OF PAST AS A QUESTION

4. fall

    PRESENT

    PAST

    PRESENT PERFECT

    PROGRESSIVE PRESENT

    did FORM OF PAST AS A QUESTION

Regular and irregular verbs

5. write

   PRESENT

   PAST

   PRESENT PERFECT

   PROGRESSIVE PRESENT

   did FORM OF PAST IN THE NEGATIVE

6. drink

   PRESENT

   PAST

   PRESENT PERFECT

   PROGRESSIVE PRESENT

   did FORM OF PAST IN THE NEGATIVE

7. ask

   PRESENT

   PAST

   PRESENT PERFECT

   PROGRESSIVE PRESENT

   did FORM OF PAST IN THE NEGATIVE

8. give

    PRESENT

    PAST

    PRESENT PERFECT

    PROGRESSIVE PRESENT

    did FORM OF PAST IN THE NEGATIVE

9. take

    PRESENT

    PAST

    PRESENT PERFECT

    PROGRESSIVE PRESENT

    did FORM OF PAST FOR EMPHASIS

10. use

    PRESENT

    PAST

    PRESENT PERFECT

    PROGRESSIVE PRESENT

    did FORM OF PAST FOR EMPHASIS

Using irregular verbs   Exercise 7–2

NAME _____ SCORE _____

DIRECTIONS   The questions below use either past tense or future tense verbs (the verbs are underlined twice). Answer those questions that have past tense verbs with statements that use the usual form of the past tense; answer those questions that have future tense verbs with statements that use the present perfect tense with *already*. Consult your dictionary for the various forms of all verbs that you are unsure of.

EXAMPLES

Did the lecture begin on time?

Yes, the lecture began on time.

Will you take the course?

I have already taken the course.

1. Did you see the dirigible?

2. Did your plants grow well?

3. Will you fly to Washington?

4. Did you eat the artichoke?

5. Will the balloon burst?

6. Will the orange trees freeze?

7. Did the student know the answer?

8 Did the sun rise at 6:30 A.M.?

9. Will the woman shake hands with her opponent?

10. Did the minister speak distinctly?

Verbs that cause difficulties

NAME _____ SCORE _____

7c There are four main points to be aware of when you write the tense of a verb.

(1) Be sure to put *ed* on the end of all past tense regular verbs (unless they end in *e*—in which case, simply add *d*), being especially careful with those verbs that you tend not to pronounce distinctly.

> When the company develop*ed* problems, a trouble-shooter was request*ed*.

(2) Be sure not to confuse the past tense with the past participle form.

> The trouble-shooter was carefully chosen [not "chose"].

> The trouble-shooter began [not "begun"] his investigation.

(3) Be sure not to give an irregular verb the *ed* ending.

> The whistle blew [NOT *blowed*] loudly at noon.

> The employees knew [NOT *knowed*] what the whistle meant.

(4) Be especially careful with troublesome verbs like *lie* and *lay* and *sit* and *set*.

Notice that *lie* and *sit* are alike: they describe a state of resting and do not take objects. Notice also that *lay* and *set* are alike: they describe the action of placing, and they do take objects.

> He lay [NOT *laid*] down on a couch in his office.

> He had sat [NOT *had set*] too long on a hard chair.

DIRECTIONS   After each of the following sentences the present form of a verb is given. In the blank within the sentence and also in the blank at the right, write the tense called for by the meaning of the sentence. Consult your dictionary if you are uncertain about the other forms of a verb.

EXAMPLE
Managers are frequently ___*asked*___ to

describe the qualities of a good report.   (ask)   ___*asked*___

1. Before a report or letter is _____,

   you should consider your audience.   (begin)   _____

2. Words for any piece of technical writing should be

   _____ carefully.   (choose)   _____

3. Successful vocabulary in technical writing does not

_____ in choosing difficult words.   (lie)   _____

4. When you _____ down to write a report, choose

words that the reader is likely to know.   (sit)   _____

5. A report that is _____ with much jargon will

make a poor impression.   (write)   _____

6. A great deal of research has been _____ to

determine what makes writing clear.   (do)   _____

7. The conclusion that short words and sentences com-

municate most easily is _____ from this

research.   (draw)   _____

8. Whatever has _____ should be

reported simply and concisely.   (occur)   _____

9. No writer should use fifteen words when only ten

are _____ to communicate the

idea.   (require)   _____

10. Do not choose a rare word, like *cognizant*, that may

not be _____ to the reader, when you can

use a familiar word, like *aware*.   (know)   _____

Special problems with verbs

NAME _____ SCORE _____

7d Make the tense of a subordinate verb or a verbal relate logically to the tense of the main verb.

She slept for ten hours after she *had finished* her last examination.   [The action of the

subordinate verb, *had finished*, occurred before the action of the main verb, *slept.*]

Having finished her last examination, she was able to sleep peacefully.   [The perfect

form of the verbal, *having finished*, shows action completed before the action of the

main verb, *was.*]

She would have liked *to sleep* for ten more hours.   [Use the present infinitive after

a verb in the perfect tense.]

She would like *to have slept* for ten more hours.   [The perfect infinitive may be used

after a verb that is not in the perfect tense.]

Caution: Avoid switching tenses needlessly in a sentence. (See also **27a.**)

She finished the examination and turned   [NOT *turns*]   it in.

7e Use the subjunctive mood to express a condition contrary to fact (often introduced by *if*); to state a wish; and to express a demand, a recommendation, or a request in a *that* clause.

If I *were given* forty-eight hours in a day, I might finish this report on time.

I wish I *were* capable of going without sleep.

My supervisor insisted that I *be given* this assignment.

7f Use the present tense to state facts or ideas that are generally regarded as being true.

A good night's sleep helps one to think clearly during the next day's examination.

DIRECTIONS   In the following sentences cross out the incorrect form of the subordinate verb or verbal in parentheses and write the correct form in the blank.

EXAMPLE

After Mario (~~studied~~, had studied) his first draft, he found many words that he could omit.

had studied

1. Mario wanted (to write, to have written) as clearly and concisely as possible.

_____

2. When he finished his report, he found that he (used, had used) many unnecessary words.

_____

3. Remembering to eliminate useless words, Mario (crosses, crossed) out "in regard to" and wrote "regarding."

_____

4. He ought (to use, to have used) "since" instead of "in view of the fact that."

_____

5. "If I (was, were) receiving this report," Mario thought, "I would not want my time wasted with meaningless words."

_____

6. After he (examines, had examined) his first draft even more carefully, he found too many weak "there is" and "there are" sentences.

_____

7. He noticed that he (wrote, had written), "There is a product available," when he should have said, "A product is available."

_____

8. "This report requires that my words (are, be) carefully chosen," Mario reminded himself.

_____

9. He realized that it is generally wise (to choose, to have chosen) the shortest wording possible.

_____

10. (Working, Having worked) hard to eliminate wordiness, Mario found the final draft easy to write.

_____

Mastering verbs: a review   Exercise 7–5

NAME _____ SCORE _____

DIRECTIONS   In the following sentences cross out the incorrect form of the verb in parentheses and write the correct form in the blank.

EXAMPLE
The writers have (~~chose~~, chosen) their verbs care-

fully.   *chosen*

1. When you (set, sit) down to write a report, always

   pay special attention to your verbs.   _____

2. Verb errors are like spelling errors: they (cast, have

   cast) doubt upon the accuracy of the report's con-

   tent.   _____

3. Writers are (advise, advised) to proofread carefully

   to make sure that they have used correct tenses.   _____

4. Attention must also be (gave, given) to the choice of

   concise verbs.   _____

5. One type of wordiness is (cause, caused) by the use

   of long verbal phrases.   _____

6. Some writers are (tempt, tempted) to use wordy ver-

   bal phrases like *be in agreement with* instead of the

   simple *agree with.*   _____

7. A simple verb like *desire* should be (chose, chosen)

   instead of the longer *to be desirous of.*   _____

8. Many reports have been (wrote, written) that could

   have communicated the same thoughts in less than

   half the length.   _____

9. Certainly the use of long phrase substitutions for

   simple verbs has (lead, led) to many wordy reports.   _____

10. Care should also be (took, taken) to choose specific

    verbs.   _____

11. A writer should always try (to use, to have used) the most exact verb available. _____

12. The verbs *get* and *make* are sometimes (use, used) too frequently by poor writers. _____

13. Many managers have (shook, shaken) their heads at the number of *get*'s found in a report. _____

14. One such report (began, begun): "After we get through an investigation of all products now available, we will get a look at those being developed." _____

15. Active verbs are frequently (prefer, preferred) to passive verbs because they result in more concise and more informative sentences. _____

16. The passive voice requires an additional verb, a form of *be*, and often a *by* phrase—for example, "Vacation policy is (set, sat) by the employees themselves." _____

17. No definite rules can be (laid, lay, lain) down for the use of the passive voice. _____

18. Passive verbs are appropriate when the doer of an action is not (knew, known) or should not be revealed. _____

19. Also, if the doer of the action is not (saw, seen) as more important than the receiver of the action, the passive verb is appropriate. _____

20. *The company gave each employee a Christmas bonus* emphasizes the company's action, whereas *Each employee was (gave, given) a Christmas bonus by the company* emphasizes the employees' receiving the bonus. _____

Manuscript Form ms 8

8

Follow acceptable form in writing your paper. (See also Section **33.**)

Business letters, memorandums, and reports have definite formats, which are il-lustrated in Section **33.** The format for an essay written in college varies accord-ing to the length of the paper. A research paper, for example, may require a title page, an outline, the text, a footnote page or pages, and a bibliography. But the average college writing assignment usually includes no more than the essay itself and sometimes an outline and a title page.

Whether you are writing for college or a career, the most important advice to remember about format is to follow the directions given by your instructor or your supervisor. Many instructors and supervisors refuse to read papers that do not follow the guidelines for preparation that they have indicated.

Usually a college instructor's guidelines for manuscript preparation include the points discussed in this section.

8a Use proper materials.

Unless you type your papers, handwrite them on standard 8½-by-11-inch theme paper, using black or blue-black ink.

8b Write clearly and neatly.

Write so that your instructor can read your paper easily. Most instructors will ac-cept a composition that has a few words crossed out with substitutions written neatly above, but when your deletions become so plentiful that your paper is messy or difficult to read, you should recopy the page.

8c Arrange the writing on the page in an orderly way.

Margins   Theme paper usually has the margins marked for you. But with unlined paper, be sure to leave about 1½ inches at the left and at the top of each page after the first one; leave 1 inch at the right and at the bottom of each page. Indent the first line of each paragraph about 1 inch, but leave no long gap at the end of any line except the last one in a paragraph.

Paging   Use Arabic numbers (2, 3) in the upper right-hand corner to mark all pages after the first one.

Title   On the first page, center your title about 1½ inches from the top or on the first ruled line. Do not use either quotation marks or underlining with your title. Capitalize the first word of the title and all other words except articles and short prepositions and conjunctions; then begin the first paragraph of your paper on the third line. (Your instructor may ask you to make a title page. If so, you may or may not rewrite the title on the first page of the paper.)

Punctuation   Never begin a line of your paper with a comma, a colon, a semicolon, or an end mark of punctuation; never end a line with the first of a set of brackets, parentheses, or quotation marks.

Poetry   If you quote two or more lines of poetry, you may indent the poetry about 1 inch from the left margin, so that the lines of poetry are arranged as in the original. (See also **16a.**) Long prose quotations may also be indented.

8d Divide words at the ends of lines according to standard practice.

The best way to determine where to divide a word that comes at the end of a line is to check a dictionary for the syllable markings (usually indicated by dots). In general, though, remember these guidelines: never divide a single-syllable word; do not carry over to the next line one letter of a word or a syllable like *ed;* divide a hyphenated word only at the hyphen. Keep in mind that an uneven right-hand margin is to be expected and that too many divisions at the ends of lines make a paper difficult to read.

8e Proofread your papers carefully.

Always leave a few minutes at the end of an in-class writing assignment for proof-reading. Few people write good papers without revising their first drafts. When you need to make a change, draw a straight horizontal line through the part to be deleted and insert a caret (Λ) at the point where the addition is to be made above the line. When writing out-of-class papers, try to set your first draft aside for several hours or even for a day so that you can proofread it with a fresh mind.

8f Endorse your papers clearly.

Instructors vary in what information they require for an endorsement and where they want this information placed. The endorsement will probably include your name, your course number, the date, and the number of the writing assignment.

9

Learn to capitalize in accordance with current practices.

In general, capital letters are used for first words (the first word of a sentence, including a quoted sentence, a line of poetry, the salutation and complimentary close of a letter, and an item in an outline) and for names of specific persons, places, and things (in other words, proper nouns). A recently published dictionary is your best guide to current standards for capitalization and for the use of italics, abbreviations, and numbers.

The most important rules for capitalization are listed below, but you may find the style sheet on the next page as helpful as the rules.

9a Capitalize the first word of each sentence (including a quoted sentence), the first word and the last word of each title, and all other key words (not *a, an,* and *the* or short prepositions and conjunctions) in the title.

> We told our instructor, "We think *How to Write for the World of Work* is an excellent reference book for all occupational writers."

Note: When only a part of a sentence is quoted, the first word is not capitalized.

> Most experts agree that workers in the twenty-first century will demand "a bigger voice in decisions that affect their job performance."

9b Capitalize words referring to specific persons, places, things, times, organizations, races, and religions, but not words that refer to classes of persons, places, or things. Capitalize geographic locations only when they refer to specific areas of the country (*the West Coast*) or the world (*the Near East*).

> Most of the doctors in the East attended the medical convention held in Atlanta, Georgia, last August.
> We are taking Business English 201 and also a course in report writing at the University of North Carolina.

9c In general, capitalize a title that immediately precedes (but not one that follows) the name of a person. Capitalize nouns that indicate family relationships when they are used as names or titles or are written in combination with names (*Uncle Ben*).

> My mother and her sister, my Aunt Nancy, met Professor Joseph Tate of the English Department and also the heads of several departments of Northern State College.

Note: Usage varies with regard to capitalization of titles of high rank and titles of family members.

Lamar Alexander is governor (or Governor) of Tennessee.

9d Capitalize the pronoun *I*, the interjection *O*, most nouns referring to the deity (*the Almighty*), and words that express personification (*the Four Horsemen of the Apocalypse*).

Style sheet for capitalization

SPECIFIC PERSONS   Shakespeare, Buddha, Mr. Keogh, Mayor Koenig

SPECIFIC PLACES   Puerto Rico; Atlanta, Georgia; Western Avenue; the West (BUT "he lives west of here"); Broughton High School

SPECIFIC THINGS   the Statue of Liberty, the Bible, History 304 (BUT history class), the First World War, Parkinson's disease, Sanka coffee

SPECIFIC TIMES AND EVENTS   Wednesday, July (BUT winter, spring, summer, fall, autumn), Thanksgiving, the Age of Enlightenment, the Great Depression (BUT the twentieth century)

SPECIFIC ORGANIZATIONS   the Peace Corps, the Rotary Club, Phi Kappa Phi

SPECIFIC POLITICAL AND MILITARY BODIES   State Department, the United States Senate, Republican Party, United States Army (BUT the army)

RELIGIONS AND BELIEFS   Judaism, Methodists, Marxism (BUT capitalism, communism)

WORDS DERIVED FROM PROPER NAMES   Swedish, New Yorker, Oriental rugs, Labrador retriever

ESSENTIAL PARTS OF PROPER NAMES   the Bill of Rights, the Battle of the Bulge, the New Deal

PARTS OF A LETTER   Dear Mr. Jacobs, Very truly yours

ITEMS IN AN OUTLINE   I. Parts of a letter
    A. Date
    B. Inside address

Capitalization   Exercise 9–1

NAME _____ SCORE _____

DIRECTIONS   Words in one of each of the following groups should be capitalized.
Identify the group that needs capitalization by writing either *a* or *b* in the blank.
Then make the necessary revision for the appropriate group of words.

EXAMPLE
(a) a class in economics at our college

(b) G̶eology 201 at m̶aryville c̶ollege   *b*

1. (a) a course in history

    (b) a course in spanish   _____

2. (a) drove north during the holiday

    (b) drove to alaska during the christmas season   _____

3. (a) representative quillen speaking during assembly

    (b) the representative from our district   _____

4. (a) responded, "you will see me again"

    (b) responded that you will see me again   _____

5. (a) reading a famous sociological study

    (b) reading *future shock*   _____

6. (a) an article in a popular magazine about psychology

    (b) "what you really want from your job" in *psychology today*   _____

151

7. (a) the age of reason

  (b) the eighteenth century   _____

8. (a) an army during a war

  (b) the british army during world war II   _____

9. (a) chicken pox

  (b) parkinson's disease   _____

10. (a) life in the west

  (b) traveling west this summer   _____

11. (a) bought gasoline for my car

  (b) bought exxon gasoline for my plymouth   _____

12. (a) the president of our company

  (b) president Adams Clay of motorola corporation   _____

13. (a) the mountains of our area

  (b) the smoky mountains   _____

14. (a) modern architecture

  (b) gothic architecture   _____

15. (a) the gods of the ancient romans

  (b) the god of the sun   _____

Capitalization

NAME _____ SCORE _____

DIRECTIONS   Each of the following sentences contains words and word groups that require capitalization. First, underline three times the letters that should be capitalized (a proofreader's symbol for capitalization); then rewrite the sentences with the appropriate words and word groups in capital letters.

EXAMPLE

A friend of mine from south america is studying geology at columbia university this summer.

A friend of mine from South America is studying geology at Columbia University this summer.

1. A student in my history 204 class told me before the spring holiday, "i hope to finish my term paper during the break."

2. The president of our college and professor james gaskin of the english department attended the annual convention of the american association of university professors.

3. Many companies, like international business machines, have research facilities at the research triangle park in north carolina.

4. The moslems who work for our corporation were given tuesday off in obser-
   vance of a religious holiday.

5. This spring we hope to see the statue of liberty and the empire state building
   while we are vacationing in the east.

6. I can never forget these famous lines from "to a louse" by robert burns:

   o wad some Power the giftie gie us

   to see oursels as ithers see us!

7. ROLM corporation, a telecommunications-equipment company in santa
   clara, california, provides a full recreational center for its employees.

8. *The wall street journal* ran an interesting series in the spring of 1981 entitled
   "the american workplace."

10

Underline words that should be printed in italics.

To show which words should be printed in italics, you must use underlining. If your composition is set in type by a printer, the words that you have underlined will then appear in italic type.

Since some of the rules for the use of quotation marks and italics overlap, you may want to study Section **16** together with this section. In general, though, italics are used for works that are contained under one cover, while quotation marks are used for works that are parts of longer works.

> The article "Work in the Year 2001" appeared in the February 1977 issue of *The Futurist.*
> Eudora Welty's short story "Livvie" is a part of the collection *The Wide Net and Other Stories.*
> "The Imperial March" is from *The Empire Strikes Back.*

10a Italicize (underline) the words and phrases (as well as their punctuation) in titles of books, films, long plays (three or more acts), long poems (several pages), record albums, and titles of magazines, journals, and newspapers.

> A condensation of *Karen Ann: The Quinlans Tell Their Story* appeared in the May 1978 issue of the *Reader's Digest.*
> *Nine to Five* was a popular movie of 1981 that called attention to some of the problems faced by secretaries.
> Almost everyone is familiar with William Shakespeare's famous play *Romeo and Juliet.*

Caution: Do not underline or enclose in quotation marks the title of your own essay or report.

10b Italicize (underline) the titles of works of art, the names of ships and aircraft, foreign words and phrases that have not been adopted by the English language, and legal citations.

> Russian cosmonauts spent 185 days in orbit aboard the space station *Salyut 6.*
> The *Mona Lisa* is but one of the *chefs-d'oeuvre* housed at the Louvre in Paris.   [In general, it is best to avoid a foreign term when an English equivalent is available.]
> In 1973 the Supreme Court ruled in the case of *San Antonio Independent School District v. Rodriguez* that property taxes could be used to finance public education.

Note: Many words that were once italicized—like *coup d'état* and *détente*—are now so frequently used that the italics have been dropped.

10c Italicize (underline) words, letters, and figures spoken of as such and special words that you wish to emphasize. Be careful not to overdo the use of italics for emphasis.

> Remember that *mispelled* has two *s*'s and two *l*'s.
> *Always* proofread your work carefully.
> The word *petroleum* comes from two Latin words—*petra*, which means "rock," and *oleum*, which means "oil."

Italics

NAME _____ SCORE _____

DIRECTIONS   In the following sentences underline the words or word groups that should be printed in italics.

EXAMPLE
In Florence, Italy, stands the original of Michelangelo's <u>David</u>.

1. The March 1977 issue of National Geographic has an interesting study of Egypt's past with particular attention given to Tutankhamen's tomb.

2. Herman Melville's nineteenth-century novel Moby Dick uses the slang expression cool made popular in the 1970s by the television character "the Fonz" of "Happy Days."

3. The word dictionary comes from the Latin dictionarius, which means "a collection of words."

4. Our local newspaper, the News and Observer, reported that Sesame Street Fever was one of the most popular record albums of 1978.

5. The Smithsonian Institute in Washington has the original airplane flown by the Wright brothers in 1903 as well as Charles Lindbergh's Spirit of St. Louis.

6. Many people forget that the possessive pronoun has no apostrophe, and so they write nonsense words like "The company gave it's [that is, it is] employees the day off."

7. The Atlanta Journal–Atlanta Constitution ran an interesting series during August 1978 entitled "Working in the Year 2000."

8. The term ergonomics, which means "fitting the work to the worker," has an ics on the end, as do many of the names of other applied sciences.

9. Someday I would like to take a cruise on the Queen Elizabeth II.

10. The first American space shuttle was called the Columbia.

11. The drama department is producing Antigone, Sophocles' play about the ill-fated daughter of King Oedipus.

12. Juggernaut, a Sanskrit word meaning "lord of the world," is the name of a heavy wooden idol with a hideous black face and a blood-red mouth.

13. My English class is reading "The Love Song of J. Alfred Prufrock" from T. S. Eliot's Collected Poems.

14. Michelangelo spent ten years working on The Last Judgment, a fresco that adorns the altar wall of the Sistine Chapel.

15. Probably the most famous single ruling of the Supreme Court was handed down in 1954 in Brown v. Board of Education of Topeka, which made segregation in the public schools unconstitutional.

11

Follow current practices in the use of abbreviations and numbers.

Abbreviations are more common in business and technical writing than in other kinds of composition, but even there only those abbreviations that the reader is sure to understand should be used. (Often the writer may write out an unfamiliar expression in full and then abbreviate it in future references.) And a letter or report should never look as though it is overflowing with abbreviations. Once an abbreviation has been introduced, the writer should consistently use it throughout the letter or report.

Figures are commonly used in occupational writing except when a number is the first word in a sentence or when the number to be used is ten or under. In other kinds of writing, figures are used only when the numbers could not be written out in one or two words (for example, 150; 2,300; $250.00) or when a series of numbers is being reported.

Both abbreviations and figures are commonly used in footnotes, indexes, charts, and tables.

11a Certain abbreviations are commonly used even for first references.

TITLES	Dr., Mr., Mrs., Ms., Jr.
TIMES	A.M. (or a.m.), P.M. (or p.m.), B.C., A.D., E.S.T.
DEGREES	B.S., M.A., Ph.D., C.P.A.
PLACES	U.S.A., U.S.S.R.
ORGANIZATIONS	TVA, UNICEF, HEW, FBI, NASA [Notice that the abbreviations for organizations require no periods.]
LATIN TERMS	etc. (and so forth), i.e. (that is), e.g. (for example), cf. (compare), vs. (versus) [Today the English forms (enclosed in parentheses) are more commonly used than their Latin equivalents.]

11b Some expressions should not be abbreviated:

(1) first names: *George* (NOT *Geo.*);

(2) titles: *General* (NOT *Gen.*);

(3) geographic locations: *New York* (NOT *N.Y.*); *street* (NOT *st.*); except for long names, like *U.S.S.R.* or Union of Soviet Socialist Republics or *D.C.* for District of Columbia;

(4) seasons, months, and days: *January* (NOT *Jan.*);

(5) common words: *government* (NOT *gov't*);

(6) books and courses: *chapter* 9 (NOT *ch.* 9), unless in a footnote or table; *chemistry* (NOT *chem.*);

(7) units of measurement: nine *pounds* (NOT nine *lbs.*), unless in a chart or table.

11c In documentation for reports and charts, certain abbreviations are commonly used: *p.* (page), *pp.* (pages), *col.* (column), *cols.* (columns), *No.* (Number), *Nos.* (Numbers).

11d When space is limited or tabulated material is given, any abbreviation listed in the dictionary is acceptable.

11e In general writing use figures only when more than two words would be required to write out an amount or when numbers are given in a series.

The *forty*-hour workweek may soon be changed to *thirty-five* hours.
In 1976 our country was *200* years old; our state, *187*; and our county, *125*.

11f In business and technical writing use figures for all numbers above ten except when (1) a number occurs at the beginning of the sentence; (2) a fraction is used alone; or (3) the exact amount or number is not known.

The 40-hour workweek may soon be changed to 35 hours.
One hundred years ago the average American worked about *fifty-five* hours a week, or *one-third* of the *168* hours in a week.

11g Figures are commonly used to express:

(1) dates: May *6, 1977;*
(2) addresses: *55* North Broadway;
(3) identification numbers: Channel *4,* Interstate *40, (919) 362–7805;*
(4) pages or divisions of books: chapter *6,* page *40;*
(5) time when A.M. (a.m.) or P.M. (p.m.) is used: *4:00* P.M. (or p.m.);
(6) decimals, percentages, and fractions: *.57* inches, *10* percent, *42½;*
(7) sums of money with a dollar or cent sign: *$520.40, 35¢.*

Abbreviations and numbers

NAME _____ SCORE _____

DIRECTIONS   Change any part of each of the following items to an abbreviation or a figure if the abbreviation or figure would be appropriate as a first reference in general writing (not in tables or footnotes). If it would not be, rewrite the item as it stands.

EXAMPLES
three o'clock in the afternoon

3:00 p.m.

on Tuesday morning

on Tuesday morning

1. fourteen thousand dollars

2. page fifteen of chapter three

3. eighty percent

4. the governor of New Jersey

5. Captain Scoville

6. Riverside Park on Memorial Drive

7. George O'Fallon, doctor of philosophy

8. the economics class in Grady Building

9. nine pounds, four ounces

10. one hundred years before Christ

Capitalization, italics, abbreviations, and numbers: a review

NAME _____ SCORE _____

DIRECTIONS   Revise words or word groups in the following paragraphs and source lines to include needed capital letters, italics, abbreviations, and numbers. You should make 25 changes. (A word group counts as a single change.) Use the style accepted for business and technical writing.

The Knowledge Revolution is described best by Robert Hillard, educational

broadcasting specialist for the federal communications commission:

"at the rate at which knowledge is growing, by the time the child born to-

day graduates from college, the amount of knowledge in the world will be

four times as great. By the time that same child is fifty years old, it will be

thirty-two times as great, and ninety-seven percent of everything known in

the world will have been learned since the time the child was born."

—William Abbott, "work in the year 2001,"

The Futurist, February 1977, page 28.

Career decision-making, whether it involves choosing or changing one's job, is

an important process. Most people spend more than one hundred thousand

hours—or one-sixth of their lives—at work. As Charles F. Kettering, the inventor

and engineer, once said, "the future is all we are interested in, because we are go-

ing to spend the rest of our lives there." Obviously, anything that takes up so much of our lives should be carefully planned—to ensure a career directed by choice rather than chance.

—Dean L. Hummel, "what should i be when i grow up?"

The 1981 World Book Year Book, page 118.

When club méditerranée sells a package holiday that takes a young french secretary to tahiti or israel for a week or two of sun and sex, it is manufacturing an experience for her quite as carefully and systematically as renault manufactures cars. Its advertisements underscore the point. Thus a two-page spread in The New York Times Magazine begins with the headlines: "take three hundred men and women. Strand them on an exotic island. And strip them of every social pressure." Based in france, club méditerranée now operates thirty-four vacation "villages" all over the world.

—Alvin Toffler, Future Shock (New York: Random House, 1970), p. 201.

The Comma , / 12 and ⊙ 13

12 and 13

Let sentence structure guide you in the use of commas.

In speaking, you use pauses and changes in voice pitch to make your sentences easier to follow. In writing, you use punctuation marks to show where the pauses and changes in voice pitch should occur. As you learned in Section **1**, the comma is the main mark of punctuation to indicate that there is an addition to the basic sentence pattern—*subject—verb—complement*—that calls for a pause or a change in voice pitch:

PATTERN   *Addition*, subject—verb—complement.

After studying the report, the president of the company decided to go ahead with the project.

PATTERN   Subject, *addition*, verb—complement.

The president of the company, *after studying the report*, decided to go ahead with the project.

PATTERN   Subject—verb, *addition*, complement.

The president of the company decided, *after studying the report*, to go ahead with the project.

PATTERN   Subject—verb—complement, *addition*.

The president of the company decided to go ahead with the project, *after studying the report*.

These are four main rules based on sentence structure that govern the use of the comma. One other rule covers conventional uses of the comma—as in dates (*May 16*, 1980)—that are not based on sentence structure. For each rule, except the last one, a caution against misuse of the comma (illustrated by a circled comma: ⊙) is included (Section **13**).

Commas and coordinating conjunctions

Exercise 12/13–1

NAME _____ SCORE _____

12a A comma follows a main clause that is linked to another main clause by a coordinating conjunction—*and, but, or, nor, for, so, yet.*

> Proposals are written by business to gain new contracts, and they are usually assigned to experienced writers.

13a A comma is not used *after* a coordinating conjunction, nor is it used before a coordinating conjunction when only two words, phrases, or subordinate clauses are being linked. (A circled comma ⊙ indicates a misuse of the comma.)

> Business proposals are written for many purposes, and ⊙ they require different types of formats.   [The comma comes *before*, but not *after*, the coordinating conjunction.]
> Proposals vary in both length ⊙ and format.   [A comma is not used before a coordinating conjunction that links two words or phrases.]

DIRECTIONS   In the following sentences insert an inverted caret (**V**) wherever two main clauses are joined. Then insert a comma after the first main clause and write a comma in the blank. If a sentence does not have two main clauses, write C in the blank to show that no comma is needed.

EXAMPLES

A proposal is a document prepared to show what a business will

do for someone and at what price.   *C*

Many times proposals are solicited or requested, but other times

they are not.   )

1. A solicited proposal usually lists what goods or services are

   needed and it states the kind of organization expected for the

   proposal.   _____

2. In preparing a proposal, you should study the guidelines laid

   down by the business requesting the proposal and you should

   submit only the information that is requested.   _____

3. Most businesses requesting proposals want to know what will
   be done and how it will be done. _____

4. Since a proposal is a kind of sales document, you should point
   out the quality of the service or product you offer. _____

5. You should also make known the experience and education of
   the people who work for your company and, if possible, provide testimonials to the quality of your company's work. _____

6. Present the facts about your company in a convincing manner
   but do not sound like a huckster selling a product. _____

7. Remember to follow the format indicated by the company
   soliciting the proposal for that company will expect to find information arranged in the same order by all people submitting
   proposals to them. _____

8. An unsolicited proposal has no prescribed format and you may,
   consequently, devise your own pattern of organization. _____

9. A company that solicits a proposal recognizes that it has a need
   but in writing an unsolicited proposal you must first convince a
   company that it has a need for your product or service. _____

10. In short, you must show the company that it has a problem and
    that your product or service will solve its problem. _____

Commas and introductory additions

Exercise 12/13–2

NAME _____   SCORE _____

12b A comma follows such introductory additions as a subordinate clause, a verbal phrase, a long prepositional phrase (five words or more), an interjection (like *oh*), and most transitional expressions (*for example, on the other hand*).

> *When our company received a request for a proposal,* we asked our best writer to prepare it.   [introductory *when* clause]
> *Following the guidelines suggested by the company,* the writer prepared an excellent proposal.   [introductory verbal phrase]

13b A comma does not usually follow a short prepositional phrase (fewer than five words) unless needed to prevent misreading. When a subordinate clause comes at the end of a sentence, it is not usually preceded by a comma unless the clause is introduced by *although* or is very long.

> *Within a week* ⊙ the writer had finished the proposal.   [short prepositional phrase]
> *Not long after,* the company received a positive response from the company that solicited the proposal.   [The comma prevents misreading.]
> Our company was chosen ⊙ *because the writer of the proposal had prepared an excellent presentation.*   [concluding dependent clause]
> The writer of the proposal sold our company's product, although more than twenty other companies also presented proposals.   [concluding dependent clause introduced by *although*]

DIRECTIONS   After each introductory element in the sentences below, either write a zero (*0*) to indicate that no comma is needed or insert a comma where one is needed. Then write the zero or the comma in the blank.

EXAMPLES

When writing an unsolicited proposal, you may choose your

own format.   ___,___

Quite often ⊙ an unsolicited proposal is presented in the form of a

letter.   ___0___

1. Even if the proposal is written in letter form captions or

headings are included.   _____

2. To make your information on costs and work schedules clear include lists and tables. _____

3. In a letter proposal you usually begin with an abstract, which is a brief summary of the contents of the proposal. _____

4. If you are able to compress the main points of your proposal into the summary or in the form of an abstract you will save a busy executive a great deal of time. _____

5. In the abstract the executive is given an overview of the proposal. _____

6. Keeping the abstract in mind the executive is better able to understand the details of the proposal. _____

7. When you write a proposal you must keep in mind that you are dealing with a legal document. _____

8. To be sure you are held accountable for the contents of your proposal. _____

9. In court you would be judged legally responsible for what you promise in a proposal. _____

10. In spite of the legal responsibility involved the proposal is one of the most specific and therefore most satisfying types of business writing. _____

Commas and items in a series

NAME _____ SCORE _____

12c Commas are used between items in a series, including coordinate adjectives.

The commas replace the *and*'s that would otherwise be required throughout the series.

       1   2   3
The office was light **and** cheerful **and** roomy.

       1   2   3
The office was light, cheerful, and roomy.

 1   2
Large **and** colorful paintings made the office pleasant.

 1   2
Large, colorful paintings made the office pleasant.

13c Commas are not used between adjectives that are not coordinate (those that could not be linked by *and*), before the first or last item in a series, or between *two* items linked by a coordinator.

A modern ⊙ chrome ⊙ rocking chair stood in one corner. [*And* cannot be used to link *modern* and *chrome* or *chrome* and *rocking*.]

The office did not lack such necessary equipment as ⊙ desks, file cabinets, and typewriters. [No comma is used before the first item in the series.]

Yesterday a supply center delivered a photocopy machine, a calculator, and a Dictaphone ⊙ to the office. [No comma is used after the last item in the series.]

Our office was now both attractive ⊙ and functional. [No comma is used between *two* items that are linked by a coordinator.]

DIRECTIONS   Identify each series that needs commas by writing *1* and *2* or *1, 2,* and *3* above the items and also in the blanks. Insert commas where they belong in the sentence and also between the numbers in the blank to show the punctuation of the pattern. Write *C* after each sentence that has no items in a series that need punctuation.

EXAMPLES
Almost everyone has to present a formal oral report.   _____*C*_____

                           1
Oral reports are used to explain policies and procedures,
  2   3
teach others what they need to know, and persuade

others to accept your position.   _____*1, 2, 3*_____

1. You need to know how to prepare an oral report how to make use of visual effects in the report and how to deliver the report effectively. _____

2. As in written reports, three of the main considerations in preparing oral reports are audience occasion and purpose. _____

3. You must consider whether the occasion for the report is business social or both. _____

4. A short report with touches of humor may be appropriate at a luncheon or dinner meeting. _____

5. At a formal business meeting of the company, a formal detailed report would be called for. _____

6. In other words, the same speech may be a huge success at one time and a dismal failure at another, depending on the occasion and the audience. _____

7. Another aspect of the occasion is the place itself: the size of the room the number of chairs and the time of day. _____

8. If you are to show slides a filmstrip or a movie, you must be sure that the room is equipped with the right kind of projector and screen. _____

9. A very effective oral presentation may be made to forty people in a room meant for thirty; but, in general, a report given to forty people in a room large enough to hold two hundred is destined for trouble. _____

10. A cold dimly lit room may also handicap a speaker unless he or she is aware of these difficulties ahead of time. _____

Commas and restrictive and nonrestrictive additions

NAME _____ SCORE _____

12d Commas are used to set off nonrestrictive (explanatory) clauses and phrases (those that are not essential or necessary to the meaning of the terms they refer to) and parenthetical words, phrases, and clauses.

> The North Carolina Technical Writers' Workshop, *which was held in Raleigh during August,* attracted middle management personnel from all over the state. [The *which* clause is not needed to identify the term *North Carolina Technical Writers' Workshop.*]
>
> The organizer of the Workshop, *Leo Bernstein,* was pleased with the turnout. [An appositive is usually nonrestrictive.]
>
> The new managers, *not to mention those who had written many reports,* learned a great deal from the seminars. [*Not to mention* introduces a parenthetical element.]

Caution: A serious error made with the comma is the use of only one comma to set off a nonrestrictive phrase or clause. When the second comma is not used, the writer seems to be separating the subject from the verb or the verb from the complement. (Remember that commas do not separate the parts of the basic sentence—S—V—C—but rather show where additions that require punctuation have been made.)

> WRONG   The Workshop which met in August ⊙ led to an immediate improvement in the reports written by the managers.
>
> PATTERN   S, *addition,* V–C.
>
> RIGHT   The Workshop, *which met in August,* led to an immediate improvement in the reports written by the managers.

Remember, then, to use *two* commas when a nonrestrictive (explanatory) phrase or clause appears in the middle of a sentence and to use *no* commas when the phrase or clause is restrictive. (See **13d.**)

13d Restrictive phrases and clauses (those that are essential or necessary to the meaning of the terms they refer to) are not set off with commas.

> The technical writing seminar ⊙ *held at our college* ⊙ attracted students from all over the country.   [The phrase identifies the term—*seminar*—that it refers to.]
>
> The professor ⊙ *who planned the seminar* ⊙ was surprised by the number of applications received.   [The *who* clause identifies the term—*professor*—that it refers to.]
>
> The topic ⊙ *"Oral Presentations* ⊙ *"* appealed to students more than any other discussed at the seminar.   [Commas would suggest that only one topic was discussed at the seminar.]

Much of the writing *that was done as a result of the seminar* was published.   [*That* introduces a restrictive clause.]

DIRECTIONS   Set off with commas all nonrestrictive and parenthetical additions in the sentences below. Then in the blanks place (1) a dash followed by a comma (—,) if the nonrestrictive or parenthetical addition begins the sentence, (2) a comma followed by a dash (,—) if the nonrestrictive addition ends the sentence, or a dash enclosed within commas (,—,) if the nonrestrictive addition comes within the sentence. Write *C* if there is no nonrestrictive or parenthetical addition to set off.

EXAMPLE

The occasion, in addition to the audience, determines the kind of

report or speech given.   ,—,

1. There are four main kinds of reports or speeches that you may

   have to give.   _____

2. The memorized speech which is seldom used in business can get

   you into trouble if you forget a word or phrase.   _____

3. Memorized speeches are used primarily by people like guides

   who deliver the same message over and over again.   _____

4. Written speeches which are often used in business may be free

   of errors, but they can be very boring when read aloud.   _____

5. A written report also demands that the room be well lighted a

   condition the speaker cannot always depend on.   _____

6. The extemporaneous speech the most frequently used type of

   oral presentation can be used on social occasions and in poorly

   lighted rooms.   _____

7. To be sure the extemporaneous speech requires preparation.   _____

8. The speaker in fact has a general idea of the content and the

   order of the presentation, but he or she does not memorize or

   write out the exact wording of the speech.   _____

9. The speech that requires the least preparation is the impromptu

   speech.   _____

10. An impromptu speech as the name implies is one that the

    speaker has not prepared in advance.   _____

Conventional uses of commas

NAME _____ SCORE _____

12e Commas are conventionally used to set off a variety of constructions: (1) negative or contrasted elements, (2) words in direct address, (3) words that explain who is speaking in a direct quotation, (4) items in dates, addresses, and geographic locations, and (5) complimentary closes of letters (see Section **33**).

> The most common kind of speech is extemporaneous, *not written or memorized.* [A contrasted element is commonly introduced by *not.*]
>
> "*Class,* would you like to give an oral presentation," *the teacher asked,* "for your final examination?" [A comma is used after the name of someone addressed directly; commas set off expressions like *he said* or *she asked* unless a question mark is called for. (See also Section **16** for the placement of other punctuation in relationship to quotation marks.)]
>
> The annual convention of the Junior Chamber of Commerce will be held at *Laguna Beach, California,* on *March 16, 1980.*

Sometimes dates are arranged differently in official documents and reports, and the punctuation then varies from the usual practice: *14 August 1978; Friday, 14 August 1978.* The usual form in letters would be *August 14, 1978.*

Note: If only the month and the year are given, no comma is necessary: *August 1978.*

Caution: Use no comma before the zip code in an address: *New York, NY 10017.*

DIRECTIONS Insert commas as they are needed in each of the following sentences. In the blank write the number that represents the reason you inserted the comma or commas: *1* for negative or contrasted elements, *2* for words in direct address, *3* for words that explain who is speaking, and *4* for items in dates, addresses, or geographic locations. Some sentences require more than one comma.

EXAMPLE
"Jim, will you introduce yourself to the group?" the president of the Kiwanis Club asked.   *2*

1. The Kiwanis Club met on Friday June 12 1982 in Milwaukee Wisconsin.   _____

2. Jim was asked to make an impromptu speech not a formal, written one.   _____

3. "Please tell us something about yourself" the president of the Kiwanis Club asked Jim.   _____

4. Jim told the group that he had moved on June 2 1982 from Tallahassee Florida to Milwaukee.   _____

5. "I am going to enjoy" he said "getting acquainted with a new town and a new Kiwanis Club."   _____

6. "I hope that my experience in computer science will be of use to this group" he continued.   _____

7. "Could you come to the officers' meeting tomorrow night Jim?" the president asked.   _____

8. Jim felt that he had succeeded not failed in introducing himself effectively to the group.   _____

9. Jim received a warm welcome from each member of the group and an invitation to the dance to be held on July 2 1982 at the Plaza Hotel in Milwaukee Wisconsin.   _____

10. Jim soon became comfortable in his new surroundings not just adjusted to them.   _____

Mastering commas: a review   Exercise 12/13–6

NAME _____ SCORE _____

DIRECTIONS   Insert commas as they are needed in the following sentences. (Not all sentences require commas.) Then in the blanks write the number representing the reason for the comma or commas that you add to a sentence: *1* for main clauses linked by a coordinator, *2* for introductory elements, *3* for items in a series, *4* for nonrestrictive clauses and phrases and parenthetical elements, and *5* for conventional uses. If you do not need to add a comma to a sentence, write *0* in the blank.

EXAMPLE
When you are asked to make a speech or report‚find out as

   much as you can about your audience.   *2*

1. If your audience is composed of friends and colleagues

   your speech can be more casual than if you are speaking to

   strangers.   _____

2. At the same time speaking to a group of friends and/or co-

   workers can be difficult.   _____

3. You have often heard it said "A prophet is not without

   honor save in his own country."   _____

4. To a certain extent this maxim applies whenever you must

   speak to an audience that is familiar with you.   _____

5. It is often more difficult to convince friends than strangers

   that you know what you are talking about.   _____

6. It requires more evidence not less to convince an audience

   of friends and co-workers.   _____

7. Since the people in the audience know you quite well they

   may not take you seriously unless you can fully support

   what you say.   _____

8. Of course an audience that does not know you presents

   difficulties too.   _____

9. Such an audience may make harsh unjustified judgments

   about you even before you have begun to speak.   _____

10. The audience may for example decide that you are too young or too old to know much about your subject. _____

11. When addressing an audience that does not know you you had best prepare a rather formal presentation. _____

12. It is important to know who makes up your audience and it helps too to know how much understanding the audience has of the field about which you will be speaking. _____

13. If the audience is unfamiliar with your subject you may need to give some background information. _____

14. It is wise to avoid technical vocabulary as much as possible whenever you are talking to a group of people who are unfamiliar with the area of your talk. _____

15. On the other hand people in your own field are able to follow a talk that makes use of common technical words. _____

16. Professionals in your own field who are likely to know the technical vocabulary associated with your subject must be treated with particular respect. _____

17. You should not define simple technical terms offer background information or otherwise talk down to an audience that is already familiar with your subject. _____

18. You will be more likely to give an effective talk if you know the kind of audience you are addressing but it is not always possible to analyze an audience before you speak. _____

19. There are three qualities described by Aristotle a fourth-century B.C. Greek philosopher that will help you to succeed with most audiences. _____

20. Aristotle said that an audience would believe a speaker who had good sense good moral character and goodwill. _____

14

Use the semicolon between parts of equal grammatical rank: (a) between two related main clauses not joined by a coordinator, (b) between two main clauses that are joined by a coordinator but that themselves contain commas, and (c) between coordinate items that are in a series and contain commas.

A semicolon, sometimes called a weak period, indicates that one part of a coordinate construction is finished and that what follows will be a similar construction relating to or contrasting the idea in the first construction.

> A formal speech is written down and memorized; an extemporaneous speech is planned but not written down.   [The content of the second main clause contrasts with the idea in the first clause; the semicolon balances the structure of the first and second clauses.]

If the second clause explains the first clause, then a colon is more appropriate. (See **17d.**)

> An impromptu speech is just what the term suggests: it is an unplanned speech that is delivered on the spur of the moment.

14a The main use of the semicolon is to separate two main clauses not joined by a coordinator. Often the clauses are joined by a conjunctive adverb like *however* or a transitional expression like *on the other hand.*

> PATTERN   Main clause; main clause.

> A written speech tends to be very formal; an extemporaneous speech sounds more natural and spontaneous.
> A written speech is suitable for many occasions; however, it is likely to be very boring when read on social occasions.

Note: Remember that a conjunctive adverb or a transitional expression is often used as an addition to a main clause; it is then usually set off by commas.

> A written speech is suitable for many occasions. It is, however, likely to be very boring when read on social occasions.

Caution: Be especially careful to use a semicolon between two main clauses not joined by a coordinator when direct quotations are involved.

> "Prepare only an outline for a talk," the instructor suggested; "don't memorize a set of words."

14b Use a semicolon between two main clauses that are joined by a coordinator but that themselves contain several commas.

If the first main clause contains several commas, it is difficult for the reader to sense the ending of that clause; thus a semicolon, rather than a comma, is used after the first clause.

> Calvin Knowles, who had memorized every word of his speech, had a bewildered, almost frightened look on his face when he forgot a phrase midway through his talk; and he stood speechless for almost a full minute before he could remember the phrase and continue his talk.

14c Use a semicolon to separate equal elements in a series (usually in a series that follows a colon) when the elements themselves contain commas.

> We studied four main types of speeches: the written speech, which is the most formal type; the memorized speech, which is first written down and then learned verbatim; the extemporaneous speech, in which a plan, but not the exact words, is often sketched out as a guide; and the impromptu speech, which is made without preparation or advance thought.

Semicolons Exercise 14–1

NAME _____ SCORE _____

DIRECTIONS Insert either a semicolon or a comma in the spaces provided within the following sentences and also in the blanks.

EXAMPLE
The most widely used speech is the extemporaneous type **;**   it

is planned and rehearsed, but not written down and com-

mitted to memory.   **;**

1. The extemporaneous speech is planned and rehearsed

   however, the actual wording varies from presentation to

   presentation.   _____

2. The speaker prepares as much for an extemporaneous speech as

   for a written or memorized one   but the speech itself never

   has a final, unchanging set of words.   _____

3. Since the phrasing does vary each time the extemporaneous

   speech is presented, the speaker is not as likely to sound

   monotonous, preachy, and uninvolved as he or she might in

   giving a memorized or written speech   but the speaker still

   has the advantage of a carefully planned and rehearsed presen-

   tation.   _____

4. The extemporaneous speech can be adapted to the cir-

   cumstances of the room in which it is presented   therefore it

   is the safest kind of speech to plan for most occasions. _____

5. The extemporaneous speech is a life-saver if any of these condi-

   tions occur: the room is dimly lit   there is no lectern, or at

   least no lighted lectern   the room is so crowded that the

   speaker cannot use a table or a lectern.   _____

6. The speaker may or may not use notes in an extemporaneous

   presentation   in either case the speaker has the advantage of

   more freedom of movement than he or she would have with a

   written speech.   _____

7. "What are you going to talk about for your oral report," my instructor asked   "and what type of presentation do you plan to use?"   _____

8. "In an extemporaneous speech I plan to discuss the advantages that advertising offers C.P.A.s and lawyers"   I replied.   _____

9. My instructor seemed happy that I was going to speak extemporaneously   nevertheless, he cautioned me not to neglect my preparation for the talk.   _____

10. An extemporaneous speech may not be written down, but it is   however, carefully thought out.   _____

15

Use the apostrophe (a) to indicate the possessive case—except for personal pronouns, (b) to mark omissions in contracted words and numerals, and (c) to form certain plurals.

Remember that the apostrophe, in most of its uses, indicates that something has been omitted.

> children's books [books *of* or *for* children]
> don't [do n*o*t]
> the class of '77 [*1977*]

15a The main use of the apostrophe is to indicate the possessive case. Add either an 's or ' to form the possessive of nouns and some pronouns. (See also **1c.**)

> speaker's duty [singular possessive; duty of one speaker]
> speakers' duty [plural possessive: duty of two or more speakers]
> everyone's duty [singular possessive of a pronoun]
> Mars' terrain OR Mars's terrain [singular possessive of a singular noun ending in *s*]
> men's shoes [plural possessive: 's added to plural of *man*]
> father-in-law's car [singular possessive; last word shows sign of possession]
> Sam's and Jane's schools [Sam and Jane attend different schools]
> Sam and Jane's school [Sam and Jane attend the same school]

Caution: Remember to form the singular or plural of a word first; then add the sign of the possessive: gallery → gallery's paintings; galleries → galleries' paintings.

Caution: Remember also that the apostrophe is not needed for possessive pronouns—*his, hers, its, ours, yours, theirs,* and *whose*—nor for plural nouns that are not in the possessive case.

> *Whose* project is this—*yours* or *theirs*?
> They put up *signs* to direct *students* to the right *buildings.*

15b Use an apostrophe to indicate omissions in contracted words and numerals. Remember to place the apostrophe exactly where the omission occurs.

> *It's* [It *is*] the duty of the president of the class of '79 [*1979*] to open the time vault.

Caution: This use of the apostrophe for contractions, and especially for numerals, is not common in formal writing—that is, in most essays, reports, and letters.

15c Use an apostrophe and an *s* ('s) or only an *s* to form the plural of lower-case letters, figures, symbols, abbreviations, and words referred to as words.

final *k*'s OR k*s*
1970's OR 1970*s*
V.F.W.'s OR V.F.W.*s*
and's OR and*s*

Apostrophes and the possessive case   Exercise 15–1

NAME _____ SCORE _____

DIRECTIONS   Rewrite each of the following word groups as a noun or a pronoun preceded by another noun or pronoun in the possessive case.

EXAMPLES
a friend of everybody

everybody's friend

the cats owned by the Davises

the Davises' cats

1. the history of our country

2. the population of the United States

3. the income of their parents

4. a poem by Wallace Stevens

5. problems of today

6. tuition at the university

7. a party given by my sisters-in-law

8. the toys of the babies

9. an address by the governor of Texas

Apostrophes and the possessive case

10. the position of the women

11. a camper belonging to Sam and Calvin

12. a reunion of the Coopers

13. decisions made by one

14. the restaurant at the airport

15. the temple of Zeus

16. the riddle of the Sphinx

17. the column of the editor-in-chief

18. the cars of Kevin and Troy

19. the picture of Charles

20. the gills of the fish

Mastering apostrophes: a review   Exercise 15–2

NAME _____ SCORE _____

DIRECTIONS   In the following sentences add all the apostrophes that are needed. Then in the blank enter each word, number, or letter to which you have added an apostrophe. Be careful not to add needless apostrophes. If a sentence is correct, write *C* in the blank.

EXAMPLE

The purpose of Mr. Alonzo's speech was
to justify the increase in the electrical
rates.   _____*Alonzo's*_____

1. In the 1980s the price of all persons electric bills will increase sharply.   _____

2. Mr. Alonzo hoped to show the reasons
for this increase and to explain the power
companys outlook for the future.   _____

3. "The power company," he said, "must
increase its electric rates to keep up with
the demand for more power to run the
many machines and appliances required
for modern living."   _____

4. "Todays home is not like the home of the
early 1900s when few electrical appliances were available," Mr. Alonzo
pointed out.   _____

5. "It goes without saying that people have
to pay for the operation of the various
appliances they dont want to do
without," Mr. Alonzo continued.   _____

6. He saved his best arguments for last,
hoping to convince his audience of soci-
etys need for electricity.   _____

7. "There are no *ifs* about the use of electricity in the modern home; its a necessity, not just a convenience," Mr. Alonzo insisted.

   _____

8. "The Smiths and the Alonzos of this country are hooked *on*, as well as *up to*, electricity," he explained.

   _____

9. "Our childrens needs for power will be even greater," Mr. Alonzo suggested, "because of the inventions and developments that will occur in the next few decades."

   _____

10. Then Mr. Alonzo explained the amount of electricity required to run each of the appliances found in most homes and presented many experts opinions of what people might do to conserve as much electricity as possible and still enjoy their radios, washing machines, and self-cleaning ovens.

    _____

16

Use double quotation marks to set off all direct quotations, titles of short works and television shows, and words used in a special sense; use single quotation marks for quotations within quotations; place both double and single quotation marks in proper relationship to other marks of punctuation.

16a Use double quotation marks (" ") before and after all direct (but not indirect) quotations, titles of short works and television shows, and words used in a special sense.

INDIRECT QUOTATION   He asked me if I would speak at the company's board meeting. [*If*, *whether*, and *that* frequently introduce indirect quotations.]

DIRECT QUOTATION   He asked me, "Will you speak at the company's board meeting?" [Note the change in person—*I* to *you*—when the indirect quotation is made a direct quotation.]

DIRECT QUOTATION   The program for the meeting noted that I was going to discuss "the effects of government regulations on the textile industry." [*The* is not capitalized because only a phrase is being quoted.]

If a prose passage that is quoted would require ten or more lines of typing or if three or more lines of poetry are quoted, indent the passage from the text and do not use quotation marks except to indicate quoted material within the passage.

LINES OF POETRY   Anyone familiar at all with the poetry of A. E. Housman is sure to remember his almost cynical advice to young people about falling in love:

> When I was one-and-twenty
> I heard a wise man say,
> "Give crowns and pounds and guineas
> But not your heart away;
> Give pearls away and rubies
> But keep your fancy free."
> But I was one-and-twenty,
> No use to talk to me.

TITLE OF SHORT WORK   Have you read the essay "Is Government Regulation Crippling Business?" which appeared in the January 20, 1979, issue of *Saturday Review*? [Note that the title of the longer work, *Saturday Review*, is italicized. See also Section **10**.]

WORDS USED IN A SPECIAL SENSE   The term "regulation" is greatly misunderstood. [*Regulation* could be underlined instead of enclosed in quotation marks. (See also **10c**.)]

16b Use single quotation marks only to indicate a quotation within a quotation.

According to Robert Crandall's article "Is Government Regulation Crippling Business?" the "EPA is beginning to experiment with various forms of 'pollution rights' in implementing the Clean Air Act." [The sentence in double quotation marks is quoted from Robert Crandall's article; *pollution rights* appears in quotation marks in the article.]

16c Place the comma and the period inside quotation marks; place the semicolon and colon outside quotation marks; place the dash, question mark, and exclamation point inside the quotation marks when these marks apply to the quoted matter and outside when they do not.

"Well," he said, "I'm ready to finish the article."

The speaker pointed out that "big business is now beginning to speak out against overregulation"; indeed, it is more than speaking out.

Have you read "Is Government Regulation Crippling Business?" [The question mark applies to the quoted matter as well as to the entire sentence.]

Have you read "Arsenic and Old Factories"? [The question mark does not apply to the quoted matter.]

Quotation marks

NAME _____ SCORE _____

DIRECTIONS   In the sentences below insert all needed quotation marks. In the blanks enter the quotation marks and the first and last word of each quoted part. Include other marks of punctuation used with the quotation marks, and place them in proper position—either inside or outside the quotation marks. Do not enclose an indirect quotation. Write *C* in the blank to indicate a sentence that is correct without quotation marks.

EXAMPLE

Gray Lanier's oral report entitled "How Much Regulation Is Too Much?" was of special interest to the business majors in class.   *"How . . . Much?"*

1. Gray began her report with what she termed essential background information. _____

2. She pointed out that seventy-five years ago business was concerned about the government's stand on monopolies. _____

3. "Then a decade or so later, Gray explained, the main issue that disturbed business was unionism. _____

4. "What is the major concern of business today? Gray asked. _____

5. "Clearly, it is federal regulation, Gray responded to her rhetorical question. _____

6. During the 1960s and 1970s the public has screamed, Give us protection from big business! _____

7. "After reading an article like Is Government Regulation Crippling Business? one sees how strong big business's response has been, Gray pointed out.

_____

8. Gray went on to report that during the 1970s Congress established a bureaucracy of eighty thousand people to protect consumers and workers from injury.

_____

9. "The many agencies created by the government to act as the public's voice have had much success, especially in the area of pollution controls, Gray said.

_____

10. "But," Gray went on, "business also has its side, as exemplified in its complaint, The standards set by government agencies are too confusing and costly to result in significant benefits to the American consumer.

_____

The Period
and Other Marks

.**/ ?/ !/ :/ —/ ( )/ [ ]/ //**

17

Learn to use the end marks of punctuation—the period, the question mark, and the exclamation point—and the other internal marks of punctuation—the colon, the dash, the parentheses, the brackets, and the slash—in accordance with conventional practices.

17a The period follows declarative and mildly imperative (command) sentences, indirect questions, and most abbreviations (see 11a). **The ellipsis mark (three spaced periods) indicates omissions from quoted passages.**

> Dr. Ng was asked if he would discuss ways to integrate visual equipment into an oral report.
> Dr. Ng explained, "Visual aids . . . often show in one picture or graph what would require fifteen minutes of speaking to explain."

17b The question mark follows direct (but not indirect) questions.

> Do you know what Dr. Ng said?
> I wonder what Dr. Ng said.

17c The exclamation point follows emphatic interjections and statements of strong emotion.

> What an interesting presentation Dr. Ng made!
> "Bravo!" some people in the audience responded.

Caution: Do not use exclamation points to make your writing sound exciting or important. Rather, use exclamation points sparingly, and only to follow those sentences that do express strong emotion.

17d The colon introduces a word, a list, a phrase, or another clause that explains the main clause it follows. The colon is also used to separate figures in scriptural and time references and to introduce a quotation that runs for two or more sentences.

> Dr. Ng explained the importance of visual aids in an oral presentation: either they are absolutely necessary to save words, or they add interest and variety to the speech.   [The second main clause explains the first one.]
> Dr. Ng named the purposes of adding visual aids to a speech: clarity, variety, and reinforcement.   [A dash could also be used to introduce the list.]
> Dr. Ng explained: "Visual aids save many words in an oral presentation. They often show in one picture or graph what would require fifteen minutes of speaking to explain."   [The colon, rather than the comma, is used because more than one sentence is quoted.]

Caution: Do not interrupt a main clause with a colon unless a long, formal list follows.

Visual aids are used for $\bigodot$ clarity, variety and reinforcement.

The colon is also used between chapter and verse in scriptural references and between hours and minutes in time references.

Exodus 5:23
6:15 P.M.

17e The dash, like the colon, may introduce a word, a list, a phrase, or a clause that follows an independent clause; but, unlike the colon, the dash may be used to set off a list or a strong break in thought that comes before or in the middle of a main clause.

Clarity, variety, and reinforcement — these are three purposes of visual aids.   [The list precedes the main clause; a colon could *not* be used here.]

These three purposes — clarity, variety, and reinforcement — are served by visual aids.   [The list interrupts the main clause; a colon could *not* be used here.]

Visual aids serve three main purposes in oral presentations — clarity, variety, and reinforcement.   [The list follows the main clause; a colon could be used here.]

Dr. Ng recommended — in fact, more than recommended — that we practice our oral presentations with the visual aids included.   [A colon is *not* used to set off a strong break in the middle of a main clause.]

17f Parentheses (1) mainly set off supplementary or illustrative matter, (2) sometimes set off parenthetical matter, and (3) frequently enclose figures or letters used for numbering, as in this rule.

Dr. Ng urged all of us to learn how to operate the various kinds of projectors (see those available in our department) while we are studying oral reports.

Parenthetical matter   Three marks of punctuation are used to set off parenthetical matter. The most commonly used are commas, which cause the reader only to pause and so keep the parenthetical matter closely related to the sentence. The least frequently used are the parentheses, which minimize the importance of the parenthetical matter by setting it off distinctly from the sentence. Dashes, the third mark used to enclose parenthetical matter, emphasize the parenthetical matter, since they cause the reader to stop at the beginning and end of the matter. (Remember that dashes or parentheses are necessary for clarity whenever the parenthetical matter itself includes commas.)

Women are more willing than men, as studies have shown, to admit their fears. [Commas would be used by most writers to set off this parenthetical matter.]

Women are more willing than men (as studies have shown) to admit their fears. [Parentheses minimize the importance of the parenthetical matter.]

Women are more willing than men — as studies have shown — to admit their fears. [Dashes emphasize the parenthetical matter.]

Most factors—such as length of flight, time of flight, and past experiences—apparently do not affect most people's sense of security in the air. [The dashes are needed for clarity to enclose the parenthetical matter that contains commas. Parentheses are also possible, but they would minimize the importance of the list of factors.]

17g Brackets set off editorial comments in quoted matter.

When you need to explain something about a quotation, enclose your explanation within brackets to show that the explanation is not a part of the quoted matter.

Dr. Ng explained, "They [visual aids] can cause difficulties if you have not practiced using them ahead of time."

A person in the audience yelled, "I seen [*sic*] it with my own eyes." [*Sic* indicates something that was said or written which is not the standard word expected.]

17h The slash indicates options and shows the end of a line of poetry when it is run in with the text rather than indented from it. (See also 16a).

Most technical-writing departments have an opaque and / or overhead projector available for classroom use.

Those who believe in the necessity of work would disagree with Ezra Pound's lines "Sing we for love and idleness, / Naught else is worth the having."

Internal marks of punctuation

Exercise 17-1

NAME _____ SCORE _____

DIRECTIONS   Fill in each space in the following sentences with the appropriate internal mark of punctuation: a comma, semicolon, dash, or colon. In a few sentences, more than one mark of punctuation is appropriate. In the blank write the mark or marks that you inserted in the sentence.

EXAMPLE

Clarity,   as well as visibility,   is important in planning

visual aids for an oral report.   <u> ,, </u>

1. Readers can study a visual aid used in a written report as long as

   they need to   audiences have only a short time to understand a

   visual effect in an oral report.   _____

2. Since the audience has only a short time to study it   the visual

   should be kept simple.   _____

3. The speaker can simplify the visual aid in several ways   by

   eliminating all but the absolutely necessary information, by using

   block diagrams, and by labeling graphs rather than using symbols

   or difficult abbreviations.   _____

4. The speaker can also simplify by showing only trends in a

   graph   not exact numbers.   _____

5. A clear   simple table is far better in an oral presentation than is

   a table with many columns in small print.   _____

6. Most visuals in books are too complex to be clear to an audi-

   ence   therefore you should resist the temptation to make trans-

   parencies of them just as they are.   _____

7. To make a transparency based on a chart found in a book

   you must eliminate a great deal of information and rewrite the re-

   maining information in large letters.   _____

8. One other criterion is important in creating good visual aids

   audience control.   _____

9. Effective visuals, such as slides and films, will help you to control an audience   on the other hand, poorly made visual aids distract from your speech.   _____

10. Even well-planned visuals can distract from your presentation if they are in front of an audience for an entire speech   consequently, they should be removed after, or covered before and after, you have made use of them.   _____

11. Visual materials that are passed around the audience can   as you might guess   be especially distracting.   _____

12. You cannot control the visuals you pass around   the audience examines them and ignores what you are saying.   _____

13. Only a visual   then   that can be quickly removed when you are finished with it gives you audience control.   _____

14. If you can change or add to the material presented in a visual you have even more control over the visual and, consequently, over the audience.   _____

15. In addition to movies, slides, and transparencies, there are several other simpler devices for displaying visual aids   for example, blackboards, posters, and flannel boards.   _____

16. Blackboards   some people ignore such obvious kinds of visuals   are a readily available visual aid.   _____

17. Blackboards offer the speaker many advantages   they are easy to use; they do not require much preparation; and they hold the audience's attention as you write and draw on them.   _____

18. They do have one major drawback   they may require a great deal of your time during the oral presentation.   _____

19. Blackboards will present difficulties if you do not draw or write legibly   if you cannot draw and talk at the same time   or if you talk to the blackboard instead of to the audience.   _____

20. Still the blackboard   even in this technological age   is one of a speaker's best methods of presenting visual aids.   _____

Mastering punctuation: a review

Exercise 17–2

NAME _____ SCORE _____

DIRECTIONS   In the sentences below insert the appropriate end marks or internal marks of punctuation—periods, question marks, exclamation points, colons, dashes, parentheses, brackets, and slashes. Then in the blanks write the mark or marks that you added. In several sentences more than one kind of punctuation mark is possible.

EXAMPLE

There are, according to Professor James Connally, certain criteria for judging the value of visuals visibility, simplicity, and control.   _—(or :)_____

1. Visibility is an obvious criterion if your audience cannot see your visual aid, they cannot gain anything from it.   _____

2. There are certain visuals for example, a small photograph, a typed page, and a page from a book that are too small to be seen beyond the first row.   _____

3. Transparencies and or large hand-lettered posters can be seen by the audience if the speaker prepares the visuals correctly.   _____

4. There is a simple rule for lettering letters should be at least 1 inch high for each 25 feet of distance between the visual and the audience.   _____

5. No rule for other visuals drawings, photographs, and graphs can be given.   _____

6. The best advice that can be given is that you should set up the visuals note the list in number 5 and move to the back row to see whether they are clearly visible from that distance.   _____

7. "How well can you see your visuals from the back row" I was asked by my instructor after I had set them up.   _____

8. "Oh, no, I cannot see them at all" I called back to her.   _____

9. "Remember the instructions I gave you," she said. "If you cannot see them the visuals, then the audience can't either."   _____

10. He wrote, "I wonder what my audience would of *sic* thought had I used the visuals I first prepared."   _____

Mastering punctuation: a review   Exercise 17–3

NAME _____ SCORE _____

DIRECTIONS   For each of the following items, write a sentence using the punctuation that is needed to illustrate the item. If you need help punctuating your sentences, refer to the rule or rules indicated in parentheses.

EXAMPLE
a list in the middle of a sentence (**17e**)

Three main criteria — visability, clarity, and control — determine the worth of a visual effect.

1. a list following a sentence (**17d, 17e**)

2. a parenthetical element in the middle of a sentence (**12d, 17e**)

3. supplementary or illustrative information in the middle of a sentence (**17f**)

4. a quotation of two or more sentences introduced by an expression like *he said* (**17d**)

5. a nonrestrictive clause (**12d**)

6. a declarative sentence with a quoted direct question (**16c, 17b**)

7. two main clauses not joined by a coordinating conjunction (**14a**)

8. a quotation with editorial comment included (**17g**)

9. an indirect quotation (**16a**)

10. a sentence that has a quotation within a quotation (**16b**)

Spelling and Hyphenation   sp 18

18

Learn to spell and hyphenate words in accordance with the usage shown in an up-to-date dictionary.

If you are a poor speller, one who regularly misspells enough words to have your classwork or professional work graded down, you should begin a definite program for improving your spelling skills. There are many excellent spelling manuals available today that make use of the latest psychological studies to present words in a logical, easy-to-learn order. You may also find the following procedures helpful:

(1) Learn the rules of spelling that are presented in this section of the book.

(2) Proofread your papers carefully at least once for misspelled words only.

As you write a rough draft, it is often difficult, and always distracting, to look up a great number of words; but you can put a check or some other identifying sign above those words you have any doubts about so that you can look up their spelling when you proofread.

(3) Keep a list of the words you misspell.

The words that you misspell on your writing assignments (marked **18** by your instructor) should be recorded in the Individual Spelling List at the end of the *Workbook*. Since most people have a tendency to misspell certain words repeatedly, you should review the list frequently.

(4) Write by syllables the words you misspell; then write the definitions of the words; and, finally, use the words in sentences.

> e nig mat ic   puzzling or baffling
>
> The poem was *enigmatic* until I looked up in the dictionary the five words that I did not know the meanings of.
>
> pro pen si ty   a natural inclination or tendency
>
> My supervisor has a natural *propensity* for orderliness.

(5) Learn to spell these one hundred words, which are commonly used in occupational writing.

absence	courteous	indispensable	prevalent
accommodate	decision	influential	probably
accomplish	dependent	initiate	procedure
achievement	description	judgment	professional
address	desirable	knowledge	prominent
annual	development	laboratory	quantity
answer	difference	library	receipt
apparatus	dissatisfied	maintenance	recognize
apparent	division	management	recommend
appropriate	efficient	maneuver	repetition
argument	eligible	manual	restaurant
arrangement	eliminate	medicine	salary
article	equipment	mortgage	schedule
balance	especially	necessary	secretarial
basically	essential	noticeable	separate
beginning	excellent	occasion	similar
business	experience	opinion	sincerely
calculator	familiar	opportunity	strategy
calendar	financial	original	succeed
category	fundamental	parallel	superintendent
characteristic	generally	possess	technician
column	government	practical	technique
committee	guarantee	prefer	tendency
competition	identify	prepare	thorough
convenience	immediately	presence	unusual

Misspelling caused by mispronunciation

NAME _____ SCORE _____

18a To avoid omitting, adding, transposing, or changing a letter in a word, pronounce the word carefully according to the way the dictionary divides it into syllables.

The places where common mistakes are made in pronunciation—and spelling—are indicated in **boldface**.

OMISSIONS	can**di**date, every**thing**, govern**ment**
ADDITIONS	ath**l**ete, laun**dr**y, drow**ne**d
TRANSPOSITIONS	per**for**m, child**re**n, tra**ge**dy
CHANGE	acc**u**rate, pre**ju**dice, sep**a**rate

DIRECTIONS   With the aid of your dictionary, write out each of the following words by syllables, indicate the position of the primary accent, and pronounce the word correctly and distinctly. (Different dictionaries sometimes vary in the way they divide words into syllables. Therefore, you may find that in a few cases your word divisions differ from someone else's.) In your pronunciation avoid any careless omission, addition, transposition, or change.

EXAMPLE

similar   *sim´ i· lar* _____

1. accidentally   _____

2. supposedly   _____

3. prisoner   _____

4. environment   _____

5. destruction   _____

6. escape   _____

7. circumstance   _____

8. surprise   _____

9. further   _____

10. candidate   _____

11. recognize   _____

12. temperament   _____

13. asked   _____

14. interpret   _____

15. perhaps   _____

16. prepare   _____

17. partner   _____

18. describe   _____

19. especially   _____

20. mischievous   _____

21. family   _____

22. prescription   _____

23. used   _____

24. hindrance   _____

25. interest   _____

Confusion of words   Exercise 18-2
similar in sound and/or spelling

NAME _____   SCORE _____

18b Distinguish between words that have a similar sound and/or spelling.

affect—effect   quiet—quit—quite
loose—lose   to—too—two

DIRECTIONS   In the following sentences cross out the spelling or spellings in
parentheses that do not fit the meaning, and write the correct spelling in the
blank at the right. Consult your dictionary freely.

EXAMPLE
(~~Their~~, There, ~~They're~~) are not many students in

my class.   *There*

1. Learning new facts sometimes causes you to (altar,

   alter) your opinions.   _____

2. You are usually (affected, effected) by what you

   read.   _____

3. Do you (accept, except) new ideas readily?   _____

4. The manager's (presence, presents) in the room

   made the meeting seem more formal.   _____

5. I am not (quiet, quit, quite) finished with my

   report.   _____

6. The (principal, principle) speaker is a realtor.   _____

7. We were (holey, holy, wholly) captivated by the

   talk.   _____

8. Some economists (prophecy, prophesy) definite

   events.   _____

9. Others have opinions that are (to, too, two) general

   to be judged valid or invalid.   _____

10. (Precede, Proceed) with caution when raising con-

    troversial issues.   _____

11. The speaker's voice was too (weak, week) to carry
    to the back row.   _____

12. She was not (conscience, conscious) of what she had
    said.   _____

13. What (advice, advise) do you have for a speaker?   _____

14. The time has (passed, past) without our realizing it.   _____

15. We were shocked by an (instance, instants) of prod-
    uct malfunction reported on the news.   _____

16. We were (already, all ready) on the airplane when
    the snowstorm hit.   _____

17. The company's letterhead (stationary, stationery)
    was attractive.   _____

18. The causes of many diseases continue to (allude,
    elude) scientists.   _____

19. (Its, It's) not surprising that we cannot balance our
    budget.   _____

20. We spend more money (than, then) we earn.   _____

21. The employees presented their (ideals, ideas) for im-
    proving the efficiency of the office.   _____

22. The (morale, moral) of the staff improved when
    their salaries were raised.   _____

23. The group did not know (weather, whether) to wait
    for the guide or to go on by themselves.   _____

24. Studying in the library has (lead, led) to an im-
    provement in my concentration span.   _____

25. Try not to (loose, lose) the appreciation that you
    have for your environment.   _____

Addition of prefixes

Exercise 18–3

NAME _____ SCORE _____

18c Add the prefix to the root word without dropping letters. (The root is the base word to which a prefix or a suffix is added.)

un-	+	necessary	=	unnecessary
mis-	+	spell	=	misspell
dis-	+	agree	=	disagree

DIRECTIONS   In the blank at the right enter the correct spelling of each word with the prefix added. Consult your dictionary freely. Some dictionaries may hyphenate some of the following words. [See also **18g(3).**]

EXAMPLES
mis- + quote   *misquote*
pre- + eminent   *preeminent*

1. dis- + satisfied _____
2. dis- + appear _____
3. mis- + pronounce _____
4. mis- + understand _____
5. mis- + step _____
6. un- + noticed _____
7. un- + usual _____
8. dis- + approve _____
9. dis- + similar _____
10. mis- + spend _____
11. mis- + behave _____
12. dis- + able _____
13. mis- + interpret _____
14. re- + take _____
15. re- + evaluate _____

Addition of suffixes—final *e* Exercise 18–4

NAME _____ SCORE _____

18d(1) Drop the final *e* before a suffix beginning with a vowel but not before a suffix beginning with a consonant.

bride	+	-al	=	bridal	fame	+	-ous	=	famous
care	+	-ful	=	careful	entire	+	-ly	=	entirely

Exceptions: *due, duly; awe, awful; hoe, hoeing; singe, singeing.* After *c* or *g* the final *e* is retained before suffixes beginning with *a* or *o: notice, noticeable; courage, courageous.*

DIRECTIONS   Write the correct spelling of each word with the suffix added. Consult your dictionary freely. Write (*ex*) after each answer that is an exception to rule **18d(1).**

EXAMPLES
argue   +   -ing   *arguing*
dye   +   -ing   *dyeing (ex)*

1. become   +   -ing   _____
2. use   +   -age   _____
3. hope   +   -ing   _____
4. excite   +   -able   _____
5. drive   +   -ing   _____
6. outrage   +   -ous   _____
7. like   +   -ly   _____
8. write   +   -ing   _____
9. advise   +   -able   _____
10. arrange   +   -ment   _____
11. value   +   -able   _____
12. manage   +   -ment   _____
13. advantage   +   -ous   _____
14. judge   +   -ment   _____
15. extreme   +   -ly   _____

Addition of suffixes— doubling the consonant

Exercise 18–5

NAME _____ SCORE _____

18d(2) When the suffix begins with a vowel (-ing, -ed, -ence, -ance, -able), double a final single consonant if it is preceded by a single vowel that is in an accented syllable. (A one-syllable word, of course, is always accented.)

mop, mo**pp**ed   [Compare with *mope, moped*]
mop, mo**pp**ing   [Compare with *mope, moping*]
con·fer̍ , con·fe̍r **r**ed   [Final consonant in the accented syllable]
ben e·fit, be̍n e·fited   [Final consonant not in the accented syllable]
need, needed   [Final consonant not preceded by a single vowel]

DIRECTIONS   In the blank at the right enter the correct spelling of each word with the suffix added. Consult your dictionary freely.

EXAMPLE
control   +   -ed   *controlled*

1. stop   +   -ing   _____
2. occur   +   -ing   _____
3. pour   +   -ing   _____
4. proceed   +   -ed   _____
5. unforget   +   -able   _____
6. begin   +   -ing   _____
7. control   +   -able   _____
8. transmit   +   -ing   _____
9. equip   +   -ed   _____
10. meet   +   -ing   _____
11. prefer   +   -ed   _____
12. big   +   -est   _____
13. travel   +   -ed   _____
14. fat   +   -er   _____
15. attach   +   -ed   _____

Addition of suffixes—final y

Exercise 18–6

NAME _____ SCORE _____

18d(3) Except before *-ing*, a final *y* preceded by a consonant is changed to *i* before a suffix.

defy	+	-ance	=	defiance	happy	+	-ness	=	happiness
modify	+	-er	=	modifier	modify	+	-ing	=	modifying
heavy	+	-er	=	heavier	pretty	+	-er	=	prettier

To make a noun plural or a verb singular, final *y* preceded by a consonant is changed to *i* and *-es* is added. (See also **18f.**)

duty	+	-es	=	duties	deny	+	-es	=	denies
ally	+	-es	=	allies	copy	+	-es	=	copies

Final *y* preceded by a vowel is usually not changed before a suffix.

annoy + -ed = annoyed   turkey + -s = turkeys

Exceptions: *pay, paid; lay, laid; say, said; day, daily.*

DIRECTIONS   Enter the correct spelling of each word with the suffix added. Consult your dictionary freely. Write (*ex*) after each word that is an exception to rule **18d(3).**

EXAMPLES
boundary + -es   *boundaries*

pay + -d   *paid (ex)*

1. monkey + -s   _____

2. try + -es   _____

3. accompany + -es   _____

4. chimney + -s   _____

5. bury + -ed   _____

6. lay + -ed   _____

7. fallacy + -es   _____

8. hungry + -ly   _____

9. lonely + -ness   _____

10. donkey + -s   _____

Confusion of *ei* and *ie*　　　　　　　　　　　　　Exercise 18–7

NAME _____ SCORE _____

18e When the sound is *ee* (as in *see*), write *ei* after *c* (*receipt, ceiling*), and *ie* after any other letter (*relieve, priest*); when the sound is other than *ee*, usually write *ei* (*eight, their, reign*).

Exceptions:　*either, neither, financier, leisure, seize, species, weird.*

DIRECTIONS　　Fill in the blanks in the following words by writing *ei* or *ie*. Consult your dictionary freely. Write (*ex*) after any word that is an exception to rule **18e.**

EXAMPLES
dec *ei* ve

ei ther (*ex*)

1. rec ___ ve

2. bel ___ f

3. ch ___ f

4. s ___ ge

5. conc ___ ted

6. gr ___ f

7. y ___ ld

8. l ___ sure

9. misch ___ f

10. sl ___ gh

11. th ___ f

12. gr ___ ve

13. spec ___ s

14. c ___ ling

15. rel ___ ve

16. h ___ ght

17. w ___ ght

18. f ___ nd

19. n ___ ther

20. w ___ rd

Formation of the plural

Exercise 18-8

NAME _____ SCORE _____

18f Form the plural of most nouns by (1) adding s to the singular form of the noun, (2) adding es to singular nouns that end in s, ch, sh, or x, or (3) changing a final y to i and adding es if the noun ends in a y and is preceded by a consonant [(see also **1b** and **18d(3)**].

boy → boys
cupful → cupfuls
Drehmel → Drehmels

fox → fox**es**
Harris → Harris**es**
calf → cal**ves**
[*f* changed to *v*]

mystery → myster**ies**
beauty → beaut**ies**
reply → repl**ies**

A few nouns change their form for the plural: *woman → women; child → children.* And a few nouns ending in *o* take the *es* plural: *potato → potatoes; hero → heroes.*

DIRECTIONS   In the blank enter the plural form of each word. Consult your dictionary freely.

EXAMPLES
day   *days*

scratch   *scratches*

1. speech   _____

2. box   _____

3. genius   _____

4. industry   _____

5. hero   _____

6. Crawford   _____

7. witch   _____

8. friend   _____

9. wolf   _____

10. ghetto   _____

11. business   _____

12. tomato   _____

13. address   _____

14. question   _____

15. city   _____

16. article   _____

17. leaf   _____

18. watch   _____

19. man   _____

20. professor   _____

Hyphenated words

NAME _____ SCORE _____

18g In general, use the hyphen (1) between two or more words serving as a single adjective before a noun (except when the first word is an adverb ending in -ly), (2) with compound numbers from twenty-one to ninety-nine and with fractions, (3) with prefixes or suffixes for clarity, (4) with the prefixes *ex-*, *self-*, *all-*, and *great-* and with the suffix -*elect*, and (5) between a prefix and a proper name.

(1) a *know-it-all* expression
(2) *sixty-six, one-half*
(3) *re-collect* the supplies   [to distinguish from *recollect* an event]
(4) *ex-wife, self-help, all-important, great-grandmother, mayor-elect*
(5) *mid-July, un-American*

DIRECTIONS   Supply hyphens where they are needed in the following list. Not all items require hyphens.

EXAMPLES
a well–spent childhood

a childhood well spent

1. a long distance call

2. a four foot barricade

3. a twenty five year old coach

4. ex President Townes

5. President elect Drehmel

6. a high rise apartment

7. a commonly used adjective

8. chocolate covered cherries

9. students who are career minded

10. the all seeing eye of the camera

11. a two thirds vote of the senate

12. Two thirds of the senate approved.

13. western style jeans

14. the clumsily executed dance

15. He is forty five.

16. She is my great aunt.

17. an all inclusive study

18. results that are long lasting

19. long lasting results

20. My small daughter is amazingly self sufficient.

21. The officer re searched the suspect.

22. a two part answer

23. The answer had two parts.

24. The up and down motion of the roller coaster made the girl ill.

25. The shop specializes in teen age fashions.

19

Learn the ways an up-to-date desk dictionary can guide you in the choice of words appropriate to your writing needs.

An up-to-date desk dictionary is a necessary reference tool for today's student and professional person. (A desk dictionary is based on one of the unabridged—complete, unshortened—dictionaries, like *Webster's Third New International*, usually found on a lectern in the library.) You have already seen how essential a current dictionary is for checking the spelling and hyphenation of words and for finding out when to abbreviate, capitalize, and italicize words. But an up-to-date dictionary serves still other purposes. For example, (1) it shows you how to pronounce a word like *harass*; (2) it explains what a word like *fancy* originally meant and gives the various meanings of the word as it is used today; (3) it lists the forms of a verb like *sing*; (4) it gives the synonyms and antonyms of a word like *oppose*; and (5) it may provide usage labels for words like *poke, nowheres*, and *irregardless* (see **19b**). A desk dictionary may also supply you with miscellaneous information such as a brief history of the English language, the dates and identities of famous people, geographical facts, and lists of colleges and universities in the United States and Canada. The purchase of a current desk dictionary, then, is one of the best investments you can make.

19a Learn to use an up-to-date dictionary intelligently.

Study the introductory matter to find out what your dictionary's guides to abbreviations and pronunciation are; to know what plural and tense forms your dictionary lists; to learn what attitude your dictionary takes toward usage labels (dictionaries vary in the kinds of labels they use, and some dictionaries label more words than others do); and to understand the order in which the meanings of words are listed—that is, in order of common usage or of historical development.

19b Use words that have no usage labels unless the occasion demands otherwise.

Most words (and most meanings of words) in dictionaries are unlabeled; that is, they are appropriate on any occasion because they are in general use in the English-speaking world. But some words have labels that indicate they are used (1) by people in one section of the country (*Dialectal, Regional*, sometimes *Colloquial*); (2) by people who are often judged uneducated (*Non-standard* and *Illiterate*; sometimes words in this category are not listed at all); (3) by people who use popular expressions that often do not remain long in the language (*Slang*); (4) in literature from past time (*Archaic, Obsolete, Obsolescent, Rare*); or (5) by people in a specialized field of study (technical words like *pyrexia*, which a dictionary labels *Pathol.* to indicate that it is a term from pathology).

When the occasion demands the use of a word that is labeled—for example, an address to a medical convention might call for technical language or even jargon—the word may be judged appropriate because the audience will understand it. But in general speaking and writing, you should depend on the multitude of unlabeled words that most audiences or readers can be expected to understand.

There is one class of words—labeled *Informal* or, sometimes, *Colloquial*—that is commonly used and understood by most writers and speakers. These words are appropriate in speaking and in informal writing and are usually necessary in recording dialogue, since most people speak less formally than they write. But, in general, in most of your college and professional writing, you should avoid words labeled *Informal* or *Colloquial*.

INFORMAL   The student *lifted* the passage from a critic he was studying.

STANDARD OR FORMAL The student *plagiarized* the passage from a critic he was studying.

Except in dialogue, contractions are usually not appropriate in formal writing.

INFORMAL   *There's* hardly anyone who *doesn't* respond to a good play.

STANDARD OR FORMAL *There is* hardly anyone who *does not* respond to a good play.

19c Choose words and combinations of sounds that are appropriate to clear prose writing.

A poetic style is generally not appropriate in college essays or professional reports. Usually such writing seems wordy, vague, and even ridiculous.

FLOWERY   He was a *tower of power* in our community, a *blazing meteor in a prosperous enterprise.*

PLAIN BUT CLEAR He was a *powerful* man in our community, a *remarkably successful businessman.*

Use of the dictionary   Exercise 19–1

NAME _____

The full title, the edition, and the date of publication of my dictionary are as
follows:

_____

1. Abbreviations   Where are abbreviations found? _____

Write out the meaning of each of the abbreviations that follow these sample
entries:

extend, *v.t.*   _____

deray, *n., Obs.*   _____

nohow, *adv., Dial.*   _____

coracoid, *adj., Anat.*   _____

2. Spelling and pronunciation   Using your dictionary as a guide, write out by
syllables each of the words listed below, and place the accent where it belongs.
With the aid of the diacritical marks (the accent marks and symbols), the re-
spelling of the word (in parentheses or slashes immediately after the word), and
the key at the bottom of the page in the introductory matter, determine the
preferred pronunciation (that is, the first pronunciation given). Then pronounce
each word correctly several times.

exquisite   _____

harass   _____

grimace   _____

pianist   _____

Write the plurals of the following words:

deer   _____

index   _____

criterion _____

datum _____

Rewrite each of the following words that needs a hyphen:

watercolor _____

selfconscious _____

extracurricular _____

3. Derivations   The derivation, or origin, of a word (given in brackets) often furnishes a literal meaning that helps you to remember the word. For each of the following words, give (a) the source—the language from which it is derived, (b) the original word or words, and (c) the original meaning.

	Source	*Original word(s) and meaning*
nefarious	_____	_____
pseudonym	_____	_____
deprecate	_____	_____

4. Meanings   Usually words develop several different meanings. How many meanings are listed in your dictionary for the following words?

discipline, *n.* _____   spend, *v.t.* _____   out, *adv.* _____

tortuous, *adj.* _____   in, *prep.* _____   magazine, *n.* _____

Does your dictionary list meanings in order of historical development or in order

of common usage? _____

5. Special labels   Some words have technical, or field, labels. These words are likely to be understood by people involved in a particular field of study or occupation, but their definitions may be unknown to people outside the field. Based on your dictionary's label of the word, what field would be likely to use each of the following words? (If the label is abbreviated and you are unfamiliar with it, consult your dictionary's list of abbreviations.)

Use of the dictionary

isochor _____

miter square _____

rondo _____

iamb _____

mitosis _____

6. Usage labels   For each italicized word in the following phrases and clauses, consult your dictionary to see if the meaning of the word as it is used here has a usage label (such as *Slang* or *Informal*). If it does, enter the label in the blank and rewrite the entire expression in standard English. If it is not labeled, leave the blanks empty.

	Usage label	*Standard English usage*
bust the balloon	_____	_____
finalized your plans	_____	_____
considerable time	_____	_____
suspicion nothing	_____	_____
speaker *don't* see	_____	_____
attitudes *get* me	_____	_____
a *hotshot* lawyer	_____	_____
do you *reckon?*	_____	_____
most everyone	_____	_____
push off	_____	_____

7. Synonyms   Even among words with essentially the same meaning, one word usually fits a given context more exactly than any other. To show precise shades of meaning, some dictionaries treat in special paragraphs certain groups of closely related words. What synonyms are specially differentiated in your dictionary for the following words?

consider, *v.* _____

sharp, *adj.* _____

8. Capitalization   Check your dictionary; then rewrite any of the following words that may be capitalized.

history   _____   pisces   _____

capitalism   _____   chauvinist   _____

spartan   _____   german   _____

9. Grammatical information   Note that many words may serve as two or more parts of speech. List the parts of speech—*vt., vi., n., adj., adv., prep., conj., interj.*—that each of the following words may be.

check   _____

hold   _____

off   _____

number   _____

ring   _____

right   _____

10. Miscellaneous information   Answer the following questions by referring to your dictionary, and be prepared to tell in what part of the dictionary the information is located.

In what year was Thomas Edison born?   _____

Where is Normandy located? _____

What was Valhalla? _____

Does your dictionary have a history of the English language? _____

20

Choose words that are correct, specific, and appropriate.

No area of composition is more important in the writing of essays, letters, and reports than diction or word choice. To communicate clearly in speech and writing, you must choose your words carefully; you must use the *exact* words needed to express your ideas and feelings.

As you learned in Section **18b** and in Section **19,** there is a great difference in meaning between two words like *accept* and *except* even though both are pronounced somewhat the same. And there is also a great difference in the meanings of *famous* and *notorious*—two words that suggest fame but in very different senses. Imagine how few products your company would sell if you used *notorious* for *famous* in your advertising copy.

> Our grooming aid is *notorious* the world over for its effects on men's hair.

Obviously, the audience for your advertisement would envision many disastrous results from using your company's product—like greasiness, split ends, and even baldness.

Exactness includes more than correct word choice, though. It also means that you must choose words specific enough to be clear and appropriate for the audience you are addressing. If you describe your company's grooming aid as making hair "look nice," you may know what you mean, but your audience is not likely to have a clear picture of its effect based on such a general description. And if you say that your "grooming aid imparts aesthetic enhancements to a person's coiffure," you will probably lose your audience midway through the first sentence of the advertisement. Exactness, then, means that your words are correct, specific, and appropriate for the audience you are addressing.

20a Choose correct words.

Remember that a wrong word is very noticeable to your reader and may, like a misspelled word, discredit your entire essay, report, or letter.

> WRONG WORDS   I urge you to *adapt* my proposal in its *entity*.
>
> CORRECT WORDS   I urge you to *adopt* my proposal in its *entirety*.
>   OR   I urge you to *adopt* my *entire* proposal.

Correctness also includes the choice of idiomatic expressions. There are many idiomatic expressions that you use every day without thinking about their meaning—for example, "I *ran across* an old friend" and "She *played down* the importance of money." As is true in these examples, the correct choice of the preposition used with a given word accounts for the expression's being idiomatic. While most of us would not write "I *ran over* an old friend" when we mean that we *met* an old friend, we might use the unidiomatic "comply to" rather than the idiomatic *comply with*.

UNIDIOMATIC   The product did not *comply to* the company's standards.

IDIOMATIC   The product did not *comply with* the company's standards.

20b Choose specific words.

Words like *nice, interesting, exciting, wonderful*, and *good* are too general to communicate clearly with your reader. Whenever possible, choose the specific word or phrase that communicates the exact quality you have in mind.

GENERAL   Mr. Chomsky's report was *interesting*.

SPECIFIC   Mr. Chomsky's report *explained the government regulations that apply to the labeling of drugs*.

GENERAL   One should study *a lot* to do *well* in college.

SPECIFIC   One should study *at least two hours out of class for every hour spent in class to master the text and the lecture notes in a course*.

Trite expressions, or clichés, are idiomatic expressions that have been used so often as to become meaningless. At one time readers would have thought the expression "tried but true" was effective, an exact choice of words. But today's readers have seen and heard the expression so often that they hardly notice it except perhaps to be bored or amused by it. Clichés of this sort are common in most people's speech and may even occur at times in the work of professional writers, but they should generally be avoided because they are no longer an exact way of communicating an idea.

TRITE   *Last but not least* is the dedicated student who rises *at the crack of dawn* to *hit the books*.

EXACT   *Last* is the dedicated student who rises at *6:00 A.M. to study*.

Note: Beware of political slogans, of advertising jargon, and of most slang expressions; they are often so overused that they quickly become meaningless.

20c Choose appropriate words.

While technical vocabulary may be appropriate for a reader or audience familiar with your field, it is meaningless to someone untrained in your area. Technical jargon, or field talk, thus should be confined to presentations made to people within one's own specialized area. When speaking or writing to a general audience, always define any technical terms that you use, and use only those technical terms for which no ordinary word or explanation is available.

TECHNICAL   Our company uses *word organizers.*

CLEAR   Our company uses *automatic typewriters that transcribe letters and reports from dictation.*

Appropriate words, then, are words that your audience is likely to be familiar with. Never use a fancy term like "occular enhancers" when you mean simply *glasses.* Avoid other heavy, ornate language unless you want to be considered snobbish and pretentious. In short, whenever possible, choose the simple and familiar word and phrase.

Ornate Words	*Everyday Words*
abate	decrease or drop
cognizant	aware
germane	relevant
obviate	prevent
salient	important
vicissitude	change
wherewithal	means
in toto	altogether
modus operandi	method
sine qua non	essential

Exactness

NAME _____ SCORE _____

DIRECTIONS   In the following sentences cross out the word choice in parentheses that would be incorrect, trite, or inappropriate in an essay written for a general audience. Write the exact or appropriate word choice in the blank. Consult your dictionary freely.

EXAMPLE

Most speakers dress (appropriately for, ~~apropos of~~) the occasion.

appropriately for

1. It is (clear, plain as day) that an audience judges the speaker's appearance.

2. Clothing that is too (faddish, with it) usually distracts from the speaker's talk.

3. The audience may then (attend, contend) too much to the speaker's appearance.

4. Clearly the speaker's dress should not be noticeably inferior (than, to) that of the audience.

5. You are not likely to have good (vibes, rapport) with an audience of business people if you are dressed in blue jeans and a sweat shirt.

6. A neat, well-groomed appearance usually helps the speaker relate better (to, with) the audience.

7. Such an appearance (attributes, contributes) to the speaker's feeling of confidence.

8. Remember that your appearance (precedes, proceeds) your words in making an impression on your audience.

9. Of course, you should try (and, to) find out whether the occasion for your talk is formal or informal.

    _____

10. Dress simply so that your audience is (conscious, conscience) of your talk, not of your appearance.

    _____

11. One of my friends' choice in (habiliments, clothes) made his audience very uncomfortable.

    _____

12. On a hot, humid night in August, he was (formally, formerly) dressed in a tuxedo to address a group at a barbeque.

    _____

13. Obviously, he was out of touch with his (milieu, environment).

    _____

14. The audience found his dress (*in toto*, altogether) ludicrous.

    _____

15. Their failure to pay attention to his remarks (inferred, suggested) their lack of confidence in his thinking.

    _____

21

Avoid wordiness in your essays, reports, and letters.

Wordiness results from inexact word choice (see also Section **20**). Few writers, in their first drafts, are likely to make the best choices in phrasing. Therefore, to insure exactness and to eliminate wordiness, writers must carefully proofread and then revise their first drafts.

Today
~~In this day and age~~ workers are concerned not only with protection from hazardous
^

working conditions ~~and situations~~ but ~~they are~~ also ~~concerned~~ with the quality of the

workplace. In other words, they ~~ask and~~ demand that work be more than safe; they

it
also want ~~work~~ to be interesting.

21a Use only those words or phrases that add meaning to your writing.

Most wordiness in composition results from a writer's attempt to achieve a "high style," to write sentences that sound brilliant. There are many unnecessary phrases that inevitably show up in the composition of those writers who never use one exact word when they can write instead a long, impressive-sounding phrase. Here is a sampling of these verbose phrases along with their exact one-word counterparts.

Wordy	*Concise*
to be desirous of	want OR desire
to have a preference for	prefer
to be in agreement with	agree
due to the fact that	because OR since
in view of the fact that	because OR since
in order to	to
at this point in time	now
in this day and age	today
with reference to	about
prior to	before
in the event of	if

Another source of wordiness, particularly in student composition, is the writer's lack of confidence in his/her position. Such wordiness makes frequent use of expressions like "I think," "it seems to me," "in my opinion," and "would be."

WORDY   *It seems to me that* one reason for boredom among workers *would be* their mistaken belief that a job, to be satisfying, must be free of routine tasks.

CONCISE   *One reason* for boredom among workers *is* their mistaken belief that a job, to be satisfying, must be free of routine tasks.

21b   Restructure sentences whenever necessary to avoid wordiness.

Often you can combine two main clauses through subordination (see Sections **1f** and **24a**) to avoid wordiness.

WORDY   Many people feel that everyone except them has escaped routine chores, and as a result of this feeling they become dissatisfied with their work.

CONCISE   Because many people feel that everyone except them has escaped routine chores, they become dissatisfied with their work.

Often wordiness is caused by beginning a sentence with *there* or *it*. When you restructure the sentence without the *there* or *it*, you eliminate the wordiness.

WORDY   *It is a fact that* all work has a certain amount of routine built into it.

CONCISE   All work has a certain amount of routine built into it.

21c   Eliminate careless or needless repetition of words and ideas.

The repetition of the same word in several sentences, unless for emphasis (see Section **29**), results in monotonous writing. The use of pronouns and similar words helps as much as anything to avoid repetition of the same noun again and again (see also **1c**).

REPETITIOUS   Even creative *writers* face a number of routine chores. *Writers* must sit down at their desks each day and work a certain number of hours at their *writing*. *Writers* must proofread and revise again and again the same piece of *writing*.

BETTER   Even creative *writers* face a number of routine chores. *They* must sit down at their desks each day and work a certain number of hours at their *writing*. *They* must proofread and revise again and again the same piece of *manuscript*.

The use of the colon and the combining of sentences can also eliminate needless repetition.

REPETITIOUS   There are two major causes of wordiness in writing. *These two causes are* needless repetition and the use of meaningless words and phrases.

CONCISE   There are two major causes of wordiness in writing: needless repetition and the use of meaningless words and phrases.

OR

The two major causes of wordiness in writing are needless repetition and the use of meaningless words and phrases.

Several popular expressions are always repetitious: "each and every," "any and all," "various and sundry," "if and when," "combine together," "return back," "red in color," "triangular in shape," "city of Cleveland," and "a total of two."

REPETITIOUS *Each and every* job involves a certain amount of routine.

CONCISE *Every* [or *Each*] job involves a certain amount of routine.

REPETITIOUS *A total of three people* complained about boredom.

CONCISE *Three people* complained about boredom.

In introducing quotations, many students tend to overwork forms of the verb *say*. Remember that there are other verbs besides *say* which can introduce quotations—for example, *explain, point out, note, describe, observe, believe,* and *feel*.

REPETITIOUS Albert S. Glickman, a researcher on work and leisure, *says,* "Work and leisure are part of one life." Glickman also *says* that "we need to improve the net quality of life." He *says* we are inexperienced in handling our leisure time by *saying:* "So far we haven't had much experience in the use of free time."

BETTER Albert S. Glickman, a researcher on work and leisure, *believes* that "work and leisure are part of one life." Glickman *says,* "We need to improve the net quality of life." He *feels* that we are inexperienced in handling the leisure part of our lives: "So far," Glickman *points out,* "we haven't had much experience in the use of free time."

Avoiding wordiness

Exercise 21-1

NAME _____ SCORE _____

DIRECTIONS Cross out needless words in each of the following sentences. For each sentence that requires no further revision other than capitalization or punctuation, write *1* in the blank; for sentences that require additional changes in wording, write *2* in the blank and make the needed revision.

EXAMPLE

~~This reason why~~ T ~~t~~he audience relaxed ~~was~~ because the speaker

seemed calm and confident.   *1*

1. Each and every speaker feels nervous before a presentation.   _____

2. In order that you might appear calm to your audience, do not rush

   your opening.   _____

3. Walk slowly to the lectern without hurrying.   _____

4. Prior to beginning your speech, arrange your notes or manuscript

   on the lectern.   _____

5. Also, take time as well to survey and look at your audience.   _____

6. It is obvious that you should establish eye contact with your au-

   dience before you begin to speak.   _____

7. Greet your audience in an appropriate way and manner; then

   open your speech on an affirmative, positive note.   _____

8. There is one thing you should not do in your opening sentence, and

   this is to apologize to your audience.   _____

9. In the event that you have had delays in getting to the speaking

   engagement, do not tell the audience about your hardships.   _____

10. It is recommended that an audience be at ease in your presence,

    not concerned with inconveniences you experienced.   _____

11. Many people feel that all speeches should have a humorous introduction, and because of this they always begin their presentations with a joke. _____

12. One should always remember this rule about the use of a joke, and it is that a joke should be not only funny but it should also be appropriate to the topic of the speech. _____

13. Nothing gets a speech off to a worse beginning than a joke that the audience listening to the speech does not find funny in quality. _____

14. Most textbooks in speech say to begin with a joke only if the joke has been fully tested. They also say that you should avoid a humorous beginning if you do not tell jokes well. And they say that you should be prepared to continue your speech immediately if the audience does not laugh at your joke. _____

15. If the point of your joke is not appropriate to the purpose of your speech, your audience may spend the next few minutes trying to figure out the reason why you included it. _____

22

Be sure to include all words necessary for clarity or emphasis.

Since many of the necessary words that writers tend to omit are needed to complete a parallel construction, you may want to study this section together with Section **26.**

22a Include all necessary articles, pronouns, conjunctions, and prepositions.

Revised omissions are usually indicated by a caret (**∧**). An indirect quotation is generally introduced by *that.*

DIRECT QUOTATION   My speech teacher pointed out, "Your body language often communicates as much as your words do."

INDIRECT QUOTATION   My speech teacher pointed out ∧*that* body language often communicates as much as words ∧ do. [Without *that*, *body language*, rather than the entire clause, seems to be the object of *pointed out.*]

Avoid using intensifiers like *so*, *such*, and *too* without a completing *that* clause; do not write *The speaker was* **so** *tense* or *The speaker was* **such** *an interesting person.* Either omit the *so* or *such* or explain the meaning of the intensifier with a *that* clause.

The speaker was so tense / ∧ *that he made his audience uncomfortable.*

Note: *That* may be omitted when the meaning of the sentence would be clear at first reading without it.

We felt the speaker's body language projected his insecurity.

Omitted prepositions can result in unidiomatic phrasing.

The speaker believed ∧*in* and made use of gestures during oral presentations. [Without *in*, *believed* would be completed by *of gestures*; *believed of* is not idiomatic.]

The type ∧*of* gestures used by the speaker emphasized certain points. [*Type* is not an adjective.]

Sometimes an article is carelessly omitted from a list of items that requires both *a*'s and *an*'s.

Effective body language includes *a* use of gestures, *a* movement on stage whenever

appropriate, and ⌄*an* expressive face.

22b Include necessary verbs and helping verbs.

Speakers have always ⌄*used* and will continue to use gestures during their presentations. [*Have continue* would be an error in tense.]

22c Include all words necessary to complete a comparison.

The speaker's gestures were as good ⌄*as* if not better than ⌄*those of* any other speaker I had observed.

Body language is as important as any ⌄*other* part of the speech.

Avoiding omissions Exercise 22–1

NAME _____ SCORE _____

DIRECTIONS In the following sentences insert the words that are needed to complete the sense; then write those words in the blanks.

EXAMPLE

Most students are more nervous about

reports

oral reports than written. *reports (or ones)*

1. The type gestures you use during a

   presentation should be the kind you

   would normally use in conversation. _____

2. Using visual aids is a means to and en-

   couragement of body movement during

   a speech. _____

3. My instructor required we use visual aids

   during our presentations. _____

4. She claimed that visual aids would en-

   courage us to move more naturally than

   anything could. _____

5. She also suggested we keep our faces

   mobile and pleasant. _____

6. Perhaps more important than any aspect of body language is eye contact.   _____

7. Eye contact with the audience is so important.   _____

8. Eye contact has and always will be the best way to communicate your sincerity to an audience.   _____

9. Remember if you cannot look at the members of your audience, you are not really talking to them.   _____

10. If you do not establish eye contact with your audience, you will not know how well the audience is reacting and understanding your presentation.   _____

23

Make sure that all parts of a sentence are clearly and logically related and that the subject, or central focus, of the sentence is clear.

Errors in unity or logic are so common and so varied that it is impossible to illustrate even a fair sampling of them. (Often the instructor marks this type of mistake with a *K*, indicating that the sentence is awkward and needs to be entirely rewritten.) But most of the mistakes of this type do stem from (1) a writer's failure to use the right kind of structure for the subject and what is said about it, (2) a failure to establish a clear relationship between clauses in a sentence, or (3) a tendency to overcrowd a sentence with adjectives and adverbs, thereby losing focus and confusing the reader.

23a Make the subject and predicate fit together logically.

The use of a linking verb—*is, are, was, can be*, and so forth—calls for a subject and a subject complement. One common error occurs when a structure that cannot function as a subject or subject complement is used before or after the linking verb.

ILLOGICAL   An effective use of gestures is *when a speaker uses his or her body naturally to explain or emphasize certain points.*   [A *when* clause is not a noun, a pronoun, or an adjective and thus cannot function as a subject complement.]

LOGICAL   An effective use of gestures *occurs when* a speaker uses his or her body naturally to explain or emphasize certain points.   [A *when* clause can logically modify the verb *occurs.*]

ILLOGICAL   Because the speaker moved his body naturally was relaxing to the audience.   [A *because* clause is not a noun or a pronoun and thus cannot function as a subject.]

LOGICAL   The speaker's natural movements were relaxing to the audience. [*Movements* is a noun.]

OR

Because the speaker moved his body naturally, the audience relaxed. [*Audience*, a noun, is the subject, and the *because* clause is used logically as a modifier of the verb, *relaxed.*]

Sometimes the use of the linking verb leads not only to an error in logic but also to a mismatch between subject and subject complement.

ILLOGICAL　The speaker's gestures were a long class discussion.　[Not only is there an error in logic—*gestures* do not equal a *discussion* as the linking verb, *were*, suggests—but there is also an awkward mismatch between the plural subject, *gestures*, and the singular subject complement, *discussion*.]

LOGICAL　The speaker's gestures caused a long class discussion.　[Gestures can cause a discussion.]

OR

The speaker's use of gestures was the subject of a long class discussion. [The use of gestures can be the subject of a discussion. The subject, *use*, and the subject complement, *subject*, agree in number.]

23b Establish a clear relationship between main clauses in a sentence; develop unrelated clauses in separate sentences. (See also Section **24**.)

UNCLEAR　Creighton Alexander lost his audience after only three minutes of speaking, and his face never showed a change of expression.

CLEAR　Because his face never showed a change of expression, Creighton Alexander lost his audience after only three minutes of speaking.

OR

Creighton Alexander's face never showed a change of expression even though he lost his audience after only three minutes of speaking.

OR

Creighton Alexander lost his audience after only three minutes of speaking. His face never showed a change of expression.

23c Keep the central focus of a sentence clear.

Adding too many phrases or clauses to the base sentence (*subject–verb–complement*)—even when they are relevant additions—will make the focus, or subject, of the sentence unclear.

UNCLEAR　Creighton Alexander, with his shifting eyes and rigid body, which showed his nervousness all too clearly, while he stood as if planted behind the lectern, failed to establish any rapport with his audience.　[The focus of the sentence—*Creighton Alexander*—has been lost.]

CLEAR　Creighton Alexander, with his shifting eyes and rigid body, failed to establish any rapport with his audience.

Unity and logical sentence structure   Exercise 23-1

NAME _____ SCORE _____

DIRECTIONS   In the blanks enter *1*, *2*, or *3* to indicate whether the chief difficulty in each sentence is (1) illogical construction, (2) the linking of unrelated ideas, or (3) excessive additions to the base sentence. Then revise the sentences to make them unified and clear.

EXAMPLE

If you decide that you are losing your audience *you should* ~~, is a good reason~~

~~to~~ change your manner of presentation.   *1*

1. The problem may be because you are not being heard by the au-

   dience.   _____

2. If you are speaking indistinctly is another possible reason for

   lack of communication with the audience.   _____

3. Slurred speech, one of the least excusable errors in oral presen-

   tations, which is a lazy way of talking that suggests to your au-

   dience that you are not really concerned about them, may

   result in the phrase *human beings* sounding like *human beans*.   _____

4. Another source of irritation to an audience is when the pitch of

   your voice is too high.   _____

5. The audience went to sleep, and the speaker's voice was so low

   that he bored the audience.   _____

6. Pitch, rate of speech, and volume are important in establishing rapport with an audience, and look closely at the people you are addressing.   _____

7. The conclusion of the speech, which many speakers ruin by suggesting that they are finished and then continuing to talk for another ten minutes, thus trying the patience of the audience, is a part of the speech that you should have clearly in mind so you can end on a firm note.   _____

8. An example of a poor conclusion is when a speaker talks for several minutes after having said "in conclusion."   _____

9. A speaker should not hurry from the rostrum, and the audience may want to applaud.   _____

10. Applause, which usually follows a few seconds of silent eye contact with your audience but which is not expected in certain situations, such as a company briefing, should be accepted from the rostrum, not from your seat.   _____

24

Use subordination to show exact relationships between ideas.

In Section **1** you learned that two short, choppy sentences may often be combined. When one of the short sentences is made into a sentence addition or modifier, the writer is using subordination. A writer uses subordination, or sentence combining, not only to improve style but also to show clearly the relationships between ideas.

24a Instead of writing a series of short, choppy sentences, combine the sentences by expressing the main idea in the main or base clause and the less important ideas in subordinate clause or phrase additions.

CHOPPY   A question-and-answer period may follow your speech. Be sure to be courteous and correct in your responses.

SUBORDINATION   *If a question-and-answer period follows your speech*, be sure to be courteous and correct in your responses.

CHOPPY   Repeat the question. Answer it concisely and carefully.

SUBORDINATION   *After repeating the question*, answer it concisely and carefully.

CHOPPY   Andrea Joseph accepted questions from many people. The people were seated in various parts of the room.

SUBORDINATION   Andrea Joseph accepted questions from many people *who were seated in various parts of the room.*

24b Instead of writing loose, strung-out compound sentences, express the main idea in the base or main clause, and subordinate the less important ideas.

STRUNG-OUT   One person in the audience was hostile toward Andrea and tried to harass her with questions she was not qualified to answer, so Andrea replied simply, "I do not have the information to answer your questions at this time."

RELATED   *When a hostile person in the audience tried to harass Andrea with questions she was not qualified to answer*, Andrea replied simply, "I do not have the information to answer your questions at this time."

24c Be sure that the relationship between the subordinate phrase or clause and the main clause is logical and clear. (See also Section **23c.**)

ILLOGICAL   Because Andrea handled the hostile person effectively, she did not lose her composure or become discourteous.   [The wrong idea is subordinated.]

LOGICAL   *Because Andrea did not lose her composure or become discourteous*, she handled the hostile person effectively.

24d Do not allow excessive subordination to make the focus of the sentence unclear. (See Section **23c.**)

UNCLEAR   Andrea, who had never had to deal with a hostile member of an audience before, showed composure, particularly considering the circumstances, which included an overheated room and inadequate lighting, when she answered the person's question quickly but politely and then went on to respond to other questions.

CLEAR   Andrea, who had never had to deal with a hostile member of an audience before, showed composure when she answered the person's question quickly but politely and then went on to respond to other questions.

246

Subordination

Exercise 24–1

NAME _____ SCORE _____

DIRECTIONS   Combine each of the following groups of choppy and strung-out sentences by expressing the less important ideas in subordinate clauses, phrases, or words. Use coordination only for ideas of equal importance.

EXAMPLE

A woman in the audience asked a foolish question. Andrea did not make fun of her or of her question.

When a woman in the audience asked a foolish question, Andrea did not make fun of her or of her question.

1. Andrea was asked a few questions outside her field, and she did not pretend to be an expert in all areas, so she acknowledged her inability to answer those questions.

2. Andrea kept track of the time during the question-and-answer period. She answered all questions concisely.

3. Some people requested additional information, and Andrea did what she promised to do, and she mailed it promptly to them.

4. Andrea had anticipated many of the questions she was asked. She had brought additional charts and tables. These helped her answer the questions clearly.

5. Andrea was well prepared for the question-and-answer period, and she enjoyed this part of her presentation.

Coherence: Misplaced Parts, Dangling Modifiers

25

Place modifiers carefully to indicate clearly their relationships with the words they modify.

While most adverbial modifiers may be moved to various places in a sentence without affecting the clarity of the sentence, adjectival modifiers usually must be placed either just before or just after the words they modify. (See also Section **1e**.)

ADVERBIAL   *When you think about the number of hours you will spend working,* you realize how important a choice of careers is.   [Notice that the *when* clause may be moved to the end of the sentence or to the middle, after the main verb *realize*, without affecting clarity.]

ADJECTIVAL   Most people *who hold full-time jobs* can expect to spend ten thousand days of their lives working.   [Notice that the *who* clause cannot be moved anywhere else in the sentence without affecting clarity.]

ADJECTIVAL   *Optimistic about the future,* most high-school and college students expect to achieve recognition and status in their occupations.   [Notice that the verbal phrase may be placed either before or after the word it modifies—*students*—but nowhere else in the sentence without affecting clarity.]

25a Avoid needless separation of related parts of a sentence.

MISPLACED   Fifty percent of all college seniors expect to become wealthy *interviewed in 1978.*

CLEAR   Fifty percent of all college seniors *interviewed in 1978* expect to become wealthy.

AWKWARD   You will find that most students are, *when you analyze their expectations,* determined to have successful careers.   [Even an adverbial modifier should not be placed so that it awkwardly splits parts of the verb.]

CLEAR   *When you analyze college students' expectations,* you will find that most of them are determined to have successful careers.

INFORMAL   Perhaps students *almost* expect too much from their careers.

CLEAR   Perhaps students expect *almost* too much from their careers.

25b Avoid dangling modifiers.

Dangling modifiers do not clearly refer to a word or phrase in the sentence base (you will find that most dangling modifiers are misplaced verbal phrases). To correct a dangling modifier, either rearrange and reword the sentence base so that the modifier clearly refers to the right word or add words to the sentence to make the modifier clear by itself.

DANGLING   *Not wanting to waste forty years of their lives*, students' interest in careers is not surprising. [The verbal phrase illogically modifies *interest.*]

CLEAR   *Not wanting to waste forty years of their lives*, students, not surprisingly, are interested in careers. [The verbal phrase logically modifies *students.*]

OR

Since most students do not want to waste forty years of their lives, their interest in careers is not surprising. [The verbal phrase is made into a clear subordinate clause.]

DANGLING   *Once unheard of*, many people today change their careers. [The verbal phrase illogically modifies *people.*]

CLEAR   *Once unheard of*, a change in careers is tried by many people today. [The verbal phrase logically modifies *change.*]

OR

Although the practice was once unheard of, many people today change their careers. [The verbal phrase is made into a clear subordinate clause.]

Note: The dangling modifier is not usually corrected by simply moving it to the end of the sentence.

DANGLING   *Having mastered one job or skill*, another one may be tried. [The verbal phrase illogically modifies *one.*]

DANGLING   Another one may be tried, *having mastered one job or skill.* [The verbal phrase still illogically modifies the subject, *one.*]

CLEAR   *Having mastered one job or skill*, a person may try another. [A subject, *person*, is supplied for the verbal phrase to modify.]

Avoiding misplaced parts and dangling modifiers   Exercise 25-1

NAME _____ SCORE _____

DIRECTIONS   In each of the following sentences either a misplaced part or a dangling modifier is in italics. Rewrite the sentence so that the part refers clearly and logically to the right word, or add the words needed to make the modifier clear by itself.

EXAMPLE
Some things have changed during the last few years *about the job market*.

Some things about the job market have changed during the last few years.

1. Liberal arts majors *almost* were certain to have a difficult time finding a job during the early 1970s.

2. Graduates with a general education were, *during the late 1960s and early 1970s*, considered to be too plentiful.

251

3. *Not specifically trained for any one job*, many businesses refused to hire these graduates.

4. Today many businesses are seeking liberal arts majors *that did not hire them during the early 1970s.*

5. *Offering something valuable to the job market*, the late 1970s began to appreciate graduates with a general education.

6. Liberal arts majors can be molded for particular jobs *who have received a general education* by the companies that hire them.

Avoiding misplaced parts and dangling modifiers   Exercise 25-1

7. *Able to adapt themselves to different kinds of jobs,* many companies now appreciate graduates with a general education.

8. Many career planning offices are, *to give greater job flexibility to students,* advising them to train for more than one limited area of work.

9. A field may be overcrowded by the time a student graduates *that seems promising at the moment.*

10. Persons who *only* can do one thing may not be able to find a job in their area of specialization.

26

Use parallel structure to give grammatically balanced treatment to items in a list or series and to parts of a compound construction.

Parallel structure means that a grammatical form is repeated—that is, an adjective is balanced by another adjective, a verb phrase is balanced by another verb phrase, a subordinate clause is balanced by another subordinate clause, and so on. The repetition of a sentence construction makes ideas clear to the reader, emphasizes ideas (see Section **29**), and provides coherence between sentences in a paragraph (see Section **31**).

There are several connectives that call for parallel structure: *and, but, or, nor, not only . . . but also, either . . . or, neither . . . nor, as well as,* and negative phrasing like *not* and *rather than.* These connectives indicate that a writer intends to use parallel structure to give a balanced treatment to items in a list or series or to parts of a compound construction.

Examples in this section are given in outline form to show the parallel structure (printed in *italics*) and the connectives (printed in **boldface**).

> Several factors have led women to seek employment outside the home:
> *their ambition,*
> *their need* for self-fulfillment,
> **and**
> *the high inflation rate* of the last twenty years.

26a To achieve parallel structure, balance a verb with a verb, a prepositional phrase with a prepositional phrase, a subordinate clause with a subordinate clause, and so on.

> Women have proved that they
> *can pursue* careers outside the home
> **and still**
> *be* good wives and mothers.

> *Day care centers*
> **as well as**
> *greater participation* of husbands in home management
> have made it possible for more and more women to enter the work force.

**26b Whenever necessary to make the parallel clear, repeat a preposition, an arti-
cle, the sign of the infinitive (*to*), or the introductory word of a long phrase or clause.**

> Day care centers are likely
> > **not**
> > *to decrease* in number
> > **but**
> > *to increase*
> during the next twenty years.

> Husbands today must cope with the pressures of
> > *their careers*
> > > **as well as**
> > *their new responsibilities* in the family.

Parallel structure

NAME _____ SCORE _____

DIRECTIONS   In the following sentences underline the connective; then make the structure following the connective parallel to the one before it.

EXAMPLE

                                                                successful
Many women today want <u>not only</u> successful marriages <u>but also</u> ~~to succeed at~~
                                                                              ^

careers outside the home.

1. In the 1970s the number of women attending college and who held jobs increased noticeably.

2. Since the early 1900s women's rights have been expanded to include voting, education, and having the right to own property.

3. In the mid-1970s women made up 40 percent of the labor force but being paid only 60 percent as much as men.

4. In the past women had difficulty enrolling in certain educational curriculums and to be admitted to certain professions.

5. Ratification of the Equal Rights Amendment would assure that all people have equal rights under the law and for no one to have his or her rights denied or curtailed because of sex.

Parallel structure

NAME _____ SCORE _____

DIRECTIONS   To make a topic outline easily readable, a writer should use parallel structure for Roman-numeral and capital-letter headings. The following outline fails to use parallel structure in five places. Revise these five parts so that all divisions of the outline will be immediately clear to the reader.

Thesis: The American worker is likely to experience at least three major

kinds of change in his/her job during the next twenty years.

I. A change in the work schedule

   A. Fewer hours

   B. Working flexible schedules

   C. Companies will use job sharing.

II. A change in the workplace

   A. Less stressful environments

   B. Recreational facilities

   C. Many routine chores will be handled by robots and computers.

III. There will be many new fringe benefits.

   A. Educational opportunities

   B. Sabbaticals

   C. Providing on-site day-care centers

27

Be as consistent as possible in the use of tense, mood, voice, number, person, and discourse.

27a Avoid needless shifts in tense, voice, or mood.

SHIFT During the 1970s women all over the world *became* aroused about their status and *express* their feelings through various organizations. [shift from past to present tense]

CONSISTENT During the 1970s women all over the world *became* aroused about their status and *expressed* their feelings through various organizations.

SHIFT First, *read* Betty Friedan's *The Feminine Mystique*, and then you *should examine* what feminists in the 1970s said about women's rights. [*Should examine* is a shift from the command *read.*]

CONSISTENT First, *read* Betty Friedan's *The Feminine Mystique*; then *examine* what feminists in the 1970s said about women's rights.

SHIFT First, we *will read The Feminine Mystique*; then the demands of the feminists of the 1970s *will be examined*. [shift from active voice to passive voice]

CONSISTENT First, we *will read The Feminine Mystique*; then we *will examine* the demands of the feminists of the 1970s.

The most frequent type of shift is in tense. The tendency to shift tenses is particularly strong when you are writing about literature or history.

SHIFT In *The Feminine Mystique* Betty Friedan *discusses* the lack of fulfillment felt by modern women and *showed* that their plight results from a failure to find meaningful lives outside their homes.

CONSISTENT In *The Feminine Mystique* Betty Friedan *discusses* the lack of fulfillment felt by modern women and *shows* that their plight results from a failure to find meaningful lives outside their homes.

27b Avoid needless shifts in person and in number. (See also Section **6**.)

SHIFT When *one* studies the history of women's rights, *we* are amazed at the changes that have occurred. [shift from third person to first person]

CONSISTENT When *we* study the history of women's rights, *we* are amazed at the changes that have occurred.

SHIFT   *Each* of the women feels that *they* have a legitimate cause.   [shift from singular to plural]

CONSISTENT   *Each* of the women feels that *she* has a legitimate cause.

OR

All of the women feel that *they* have a legitimate cause.

27c Avoid needless shifts from indirect to direct discourse.

SHIFT   Women are now asking *that they be paid* the same salaries as men are paid for equivalent jobs and *can they enter* the same professions that men do?   [shift from declarative sentence structure to interrogative sentence structure]

CONSISTENT   Women are now asking *that they be paid* the same salaries as men are paid for equivalent jobs and *that they be permitted* to enter the same professions that men enter.

OR

Women are now asking, "*Can we be paid* the same salaries as men are paid for equivalent jobs and *be permitted* to enter the same professions that men enter?"

Avoiding needless shifts

Exercise 27–1

NAME _____ SCORE _____

DIRECTIONS   In each of the following sentences, indicate the kind of shift by writing *1* if the shift is in tense, mood, or voice; *2* if it is in person or number; or *3* if it is from indirect to direct discourse. Then revise the sentence to eliminate the needless shift.

EXAMPLE

When ~~one~~ look͟s̸ back over history, we realize how much the

     ^we

role of women in society has changed.   _2_

1. In most ancient societies women remained at home, and no

   formal education was received by them.   _____

2. Roman women had more legal rights and social freedom than

   other European women did, but their status decreases with the

   spread of Christianity.   _____

3. Examine Old Testament tradition, and you should see why the

   Church affirmed the dominant role of men.   _____

4. Indeed, most of the world's religions questioned the equality

   of women, and could they do any useful work other than

   housework and child rearing?   _____

5. Before the 1800s very few women in the United States worked

   outside the home, and those who did often do so out of neces-

   sity.   _____

6. When we examine the course of the Industrial Revolution, you
   find that one of its results was the emergence of women as a
   significant part of the work force. _____

7. At first the working conditions in textile mills and in other factories that employed women were reasonably good, but as time
   goes by conditions worsen and salaries drop. _____

8. The women's rights movement, which began during the first
   half of the 1800s, makes progress with the introduction of a con-
   stitutional amendment granting women the right to vote. _____

9. Beginning in 1878 the amendment was brought before Congress every year until it finally passes in 1920. _____

10. Each of the major wars fought by our country has also had their
    effect on the role of women outside the home. _____

28

Make each pronoun refer unmistakably to its antecedent.

A pronoun has no real meaning of its own; rather, it depends on its antecedent—the word it refers to—for its meaning. If a pronoun does not have a clear reference, then the reader does not know what the pronoun means. And if a pronoun refers to the general idea of the preceding sentence or sentences, the reader may have difficulty determining the pronoun's meaning.

> *They* claim that the standard workweek will be only thirty-five hours by the middle of the 1980s. *They* say *this* because *it* has decreased continually since 1900.

There are three main ways to correct an unclear reference of a pronoun: (1) rewrite the sentence to eliminate the pronoun; (2) provide a clear antecedent for the pronoun to refer to; and (3) substitute a noun for the pronoun or, in the case of *this*, add a noun, making the pronoun an adjective.

> *A report produced by the American Institute for Research* claims that the standard workweek will be only thirty-five hours by the middle of the 1980s. *The researchers who worked on the report* make *this claim* because the *workweek* has decreased continually since 1900.

28a Avoid ambiguous references.

AMBIGUOUS John told Oliver that *he* had a new job.

CLEAR John told Oliver, "*I* have a new job."
OR
John told Oliver, "*You* have a new job."

28b Avoid remote or obscure references.

REMOTE Oliver studied the job description. A variety of skills and a considerable amount of work experience were required. *It* convinced Oliver that he was not qualified for the position.

CLEAR Oliver studied the job description. A variety of skills and a considerable amount of work experience were required. The *job description* convinced Oliver that he was not qualified for the position.

OBSCURE When *Mrs. Mazaki's* company was founded, *she* asked Oliver to join her staff. [A reference to an antecedent in the possessive case is unclear.]

CLEAR When *Mrs. Mazaki* founded her company, *she* asked Oliver to join her staff.

28c In general, avoid broad references—that is, the use of pronouns like *which, it,* and *this*—to refer to the general idea of a preceding sentence or clause.

BROAD   Oliver was a skillful writer, and he used *it* to get ahead in the new company.

CLEAR   Oliver used his *writing skill* to get ahead in the new company.

BROAD   The new company sent out many proposals. *This* was Oliver's specialty.

CLEAR   The new company sent out many proposals. *This type of writing* was Oliver's specialty.   [One way to correct a vague *this* is to add a noun for the pronoun to modify.]

OR

The new company's need to submit many proposals made use of Oliver's specialty.   [The vague *this* is eliminated by rewriting the two sentences as one.]

28d Avoid the awkward placement of the pronoun *it* near the expletive *it* and the awkward use of *it* to refer to a preceding noun.

AWKWARD   Although *it* was difficult for Oliver to get a new job, he decided to do *it*.   [The use of the first *it*—an expletive—makes the meaning of the second *it*—a pronoun—unclear.]

CLEAR   Although *it* was difficult for Oliver to get a new job, he decided to *do so*.

AWKWARD   In the yellow pages *it lists* the names of all insurance companies in the area.   [This construction is wordy as well as awkward.]

CLEAR   The *yellow pages list* the names of all insurance companies in the area.

Reference of pronouns   Exercise 28–1

NAME _____ SCORE _____

DIRECTIONS   In the following sentences mark a capital *V* through each pronoun whose reference is vague and write the pronoun in the blank. Then revise the sentence or sentences to clarify the meaning.

EXAMPLE

t The number of hours spent at work may lessen dur-

Because

ing the coming decade, ~~which will cause~~ people

will

~~to~~ reevaluate their idea of leisure time.   *which*

1. The four-day work week is used by some companies.

   This gives employees more leisure time.   _____

2. Increased automation is bound to give employees

   more leisure time. It is not known what employees

   will do with it.   _____

3. In Sebastian de Grazia's *Of Time, Work and*

   Leisure he explains the ancient and modern at-

   titudes toward leisure.   _____

4. The ancient Greeks had a different notion of leisure

   from ours. We think of using our leisure time to ac-

   complish a definite task, like painting our house or

   washing our car. To them it meant doing something

   enjoyable for its own sake.   _____

5. Many Americans are totally dedicated to the work ethic. This causes them to take a second job if they have very much spare time.

        _____

6. When Americans retire from their careers, they often do not know what to do with it.

        _____

7. Although it has been a tradition in our country to retire at the age of sixty-five, we are now unsure that it is a good thing.

        _____

8. Many people find nothing to give them a sense of fulfillment outside their work, which leads to personal unhappiness and maladjustment.

        _____

9. Perhaps we need to adopt the ancient Greek attitude toward leisure. They thought that writing poetry, painting, thinking, or even doing nothing could be desirable goals in themselves.

        _____

10. Automation may well allow us to have three days off during each week and to have ten or more years of retirement living. We must educate ourselves to use this creatively.

        _____

29

When appropriate, arrange the parts of the sentence, and the sentences in a paragraph, to emphasize important ideas.

On occasion you may want to emphasize certain points in your essays and reports. Of the many ways to achieve emphasis, four are especially helpful.

29a Gain emphasis by placing important words at the beginning or at the end of the sentence—especially at the end—and unimportant words in the middle.

NATURAL   *Leisure time can be a problem*, sociologists tell us.

EMPHATIC   *Leisure time*, sociologists tell us, *can be a problem*.

29b Gain emphasis by using the active voice.

PASSIVE   Most people's leisure time *is spent* watching television.

ACTIVE   Most people *spend* their leisure time watching television.

29c Gain emphasis by repeating words or structures. (See also Section **26.**)

UNEMPHATIC   Retirement has many unpleasant associations for a person who has no interests outside work. It makes the person think of boredom. And it may also bring to mind uselessness and loss of self-respect.

EMPHATIC   Retirement has many unpleasant *associations* for a person who has no interests outside his or her work—*associations* such as *boredom, uselessness,* and *loss of self-respect.*

29d Gain emphasis by writing the main ideas in sentences that are noticeably shorter than the other sentences.

[1]"Stopping out," or taking a temporary leave from college, is not a new phenomenon, but it is a practice that is gaining popularity among college students. [2]One national survey shows that 95 percent of all college students have seriously considered stopping out during their undergraduate years. [3]Many students would like to leave school temporarily to travel, to work, or just to find themselves. [4]They feel that what they learn during their absence from college will introduce them to the real world, will motivate them to become better students, and will enable them to set realistic goals for their futures. [5]*Certainly stopping out can do all of these things.*

[6]College administrators and many students who have unsuccessfully tried stopping out warn about the disadvantages: getting permanently sidetracked from one's education, finding that travel plans and jobs do not always work out, being tempted to do nothing during the absence from college. [7]*Thus, stopping out is not to be tried on impulse.* [8]It requires careful planning so that a student will not waste a semester or a year, and it requires informing advisors and filling out forms so that the college will

know what the student will be doing during the leave and when he or she will be returning.

Note: These two paragraphs also illustrate the use of the active voice—in all sentences—and parallel structure—in sentences 3, 4, and 6—to achieve emphasis.

Emphasis

NAME _____ SCORE _____

DIRECTIONS   Rewrite each of the following sentences to achieve emphasis. (In the case of the last item, you will need to rewrite only one of the sentences—the one that you feel should be emphasized.) After your revision, show what you did to achieve emphasis by writing the rule letter from Section 29—*a*, *b*, *c*, or *d*—that applies to your revision.

EXAMPLE
How many people look forward to retirement, one wonders.

How many people, one wonders, look foward to retirement? a

1. One survey found that more than 80 percent of all workers would go on working after retirement if they could.

2. The jobs held by two-thirds of these same workers were not liked by them.

3. They wished to work at a small business of their own instead of working at their current jobs.

4. Many people think of work as something they must do. Something they do not want to do is also their definition of work.

5. American workers have never had more free time than they do today, spending less than one-fourth of their hours on the job as compared to the one-third work allotment of the early 1900s. Indeed, the workweek has steadily decreased from the 53-hour work schedule of 1900, to the 40-hour workweek of 1970, to a probable 35-hour workweek by 1985. Ironically, though, Americans have never expressed more displeasure with their jobs than they do today, with fully 44 percent of those surveyed in a recent poll by *Psychology Today* expressing the feeling that they were "locked into" or trapped in their work. With a greater amount of time to do what they want to do, one would expect happier workers, but maybe more leisure time is not the way to happiness after all.

30

Vary the length, structure, and beginnings of sentences to create a pleasing style.

A writer of essays is usually more concerned about variety than a writer of business letters and reports is. In occupational writing, quite understandably, the emphasis is on clarity and simplicity rather than on style. But even the occupational writer, to hold the reader's attention, must not rely too much on short, choppy sentences, on strung-out compound sentences, or on sentences that always begin with the subject. In short, business and technical writers, as well as general writers, need to know how to vary their sentence structure to produce composition that is not only clear but also pleasing to read.

30a Vary the length of sentences, using short sentences primarily for emphasis. (See **29d.**)

30b Vary the structure of sentences. (See also **1f** and Section **24.**)

As you learned in Section **24,** too many short, simple sentences produce an immature style, as does an overuse of stringy compound sentences. There are more complex sentences (sentences with subordinate clauses) in effective composition than there are simple and compound sentences combined.

SIMPLE   A few companies have set up retirement clinics. These clinics help workers prepare for their retirement years.

COMPOUND   A few companies have set up retirement clinics, and these clinics help workers prepare for their retirement years.

COMPLEX   A few companies have set up retirement clinics that help workers prepare for their retirement years.

30c Vary the beginnings of sentences.

(1) Begin with a modifier.

Gradually, workers learn to cope with retirement.

(2) Begin with a phrase.

Through courses and counseling, the clinics help people discover the talents they would like to develop.

(3) Begin with a subordinate clause.

Because more and more people are reaching retirement age, these clinics may become commonplace in the future.

(4) Begin with a coordinating conjunction or a transitional expression when the word or phrase can be used to show the proper relationship between sentences.

> More people are reaching retirement age in our country than ever before. *And* [or *In addition*,] many employees are retiring at the age of fifty-five or earlier.

30d Occasionally vary from subject-verb-complement word order by inserting a word or words between two of these parts.

> s-v-c   Many employees are retiring at the age of fifty-five.
>
> VARIED   Many employees, *at the age of fifty-five*, are retiring.

Note: This kind of variety must be used with discretion because too frequent a separation of sentence parts makes the writer's style unnatural and even difficult to follow. (See also **25a**.)

30e Occasionally use an interrogative, imperative, or exclamatory sentence to vary from the more common declarative sentence.

> Retirement clinics are not commonplace today. In fact, only a very few companies supply them. *But who can say how popular they may become in the next twenty years when the greatest percentage of workers in our history will be reaching retirement age?*

Variety   Exercise 30-1

NAME _____ SCORE _____

DIRECTIONS   Analyze the ways in which the following paragraphs achieve variety by answering the questions printed below.

[1] Until two weeks ago I had not watched a superhero in action since I was a child awe-struck by the Saturday-morning serial at the local theater. [2] To pacify my two young sons, I agreed to watch one installment of their favorite kiddie show—"The Super Friends." [3] "But only one show," I assured them, afraid that they would expect me to get up every Saturday morning at 8:00.

[4] As the superheroes—Superman, Batman, Wonder Woman, and Aquaman—zoomed across the television screen, I sank back in my pillow, prepared to bite my tongue to keep from laughing at or making some insulting remark about my children's heroes. [5] The first episode went by very quickly. [6] After two encounters with their adversary, Superman and Wonder Woman subdued Dr. Fright by exposing him to his own remarkable invention—fear gas, which he had been spewing from a futuristic blimp on the helpless citizens of our nation's largest city. [7] Surprisingly, I did not have to bite my tongue. [8] And I didn't laugh either. [9] "What's wrong with me?" I puzzled when I secretly cheered along with my boys at Superman and Wonder Woman's success. [10] "I'm an adult. [11] I'm an educated person. [12] I teach students great literature like *Death of a Salesman*, 'The Death of Ivan Ilyitch,' and *As I Lay Dying*." [13] I tried to mentally whip myself back into shape. [14] "How can I possibly tolerate a show that exhibits all the characteristics of bad writing—the trite plot, the stereotyped characters, and the inevitable poetic justice?" [15] Yet there I was, enjoying the very kind of literature I exposed to folly in my freshman English classes. [16] How could I possibly have lost all sense of literary judgment?

[17] Obviously, I am no different from my children, who have not yet learned to appreciate great literature. [18] I still like to see a super kind of person win out against impossible odds. [19] I've become tired of characters like myself who just endure or, a little better, as William Faulkner would put it, "prevail." [20] There are

too many heroes in real life and in literature who lose—who get shot or exposed for their weaknesses or who simply have a hard time breathing the air or drinking the water. [21] So bring on the superheroes! [22] They have a chance to win.

1. Which sentences are shorter than the others? _____

   Why do you think the writer used them?

2. How many simple sentences are there? _____

   How many compound sentences? _____

   How many complex sentences? _____

3. How many sentences begin with something other than the subject? _____

   Which sentences begin with an adverb or an adverb phrase? _____

   Which with an adverb clause? _____

   Which with a coordinating conjunction or transitional expression? _____

4. Which sentences are not declarative sentences? _____

   What kind are they? _____

Variety   Exercise 30–2

NAME _____ SCORE _____

DIRECTIONS   Write sentences to illustrate the techniques for achieving variety listed below. You may want to continue this book's theme of the world of work.

1. two sentences, the second beginning with a coordinating conjunction

2. a sentence beginning with a subordinate clause

3. a sentence beginning with a phrase

4. a sentence beginning with a single modifier

5. a sentence in which two of the basic sentence parts (subject-verb-complement) are separated by an intervening word or words

275

Mastering variety: a review Exercise 30–3

NAME _____

DIRECTIONS   Rewrite the following paragraph so that the sentences flow more smoothly and the style is more varied: use a transitional expression or two and vary the beginnings of a few sentences through subordination.

[1] We can find evidence of a worthwhile use of leisure time in our society. [2] The arts are experiencing an unusual amount of participation and appreciation. [3] People are painting, writing, dancing, and making music as never before. [4] Small rural communities are being visited by symphony orchestras and art exhibitions. [5] The art of handicrafts, especially, is flourishing everywhere. [6] A few areas have a majority of their citizens involved in making things. [7] They are making things like pottery, furniture, and macramé items. [8] People are buying the works that are produced. [9] Artists of all types are able to make a living from their crafts.

Revision

The Paragraph ¶ 31

31

Write unified, coherent, and adequately developed paragraphs.

We recognize the beginning of a new paragraph in a composition by the indention—about one-half inch or five typewriter spaces—of the first word. Although a paragraph may be only one sentence long, most paragraphs require several sentences to develop adequately the central, or controlling, idea. We expect, by the time we finish reading the paragraph, to know what the writer's controlling idea is and to be able to recognize the relationship that each of the other sentences has to the sentence that states or suggests this controlling idea. And, finally, we expect the sentences to flow along smoothly so we do not have to mentally fill in any words or phrases or stop reading after every sentence or two to refocus our attention.

31a Make each sentence in the paragraph contribute to the controlling idea.

The controlling idea is printed in italics in the following paragraph. Notice that the key word, *flextime*, is echoed in each of the other sentences in the paragraph. (The words that echo *flextime* are printed in boldface.)

[1] *Flextime is here to stay.* [2] Surveys, like one conducted by *Psychology Today* in 1978, suggest that the American worker strongly approves of **flextime**; fully 78 percent of those questioned by *Psychology Today* wanted to have **some say** in the time they started and finished their workday. [3] Employers, while they acknowledge some problems with **individualized work schedules**, seem equally satisfied with the system; as proof, only two percent of the companies that have tried **flextime** have returned to eight- or nine-to-five schedules. [4] Based, then, on present trends, **flextime** seems certain to replace the rigid work schedules that people have followed since the outset of the Industrial Revolution. [5] Looking ahead to the kind of workplace we will have in the year 2001, William Abbott, editor of the World Future Society's newsletter, *Careers Tomorrow*, says quite confidently, "Workers will schedule their own hours under **flextime**."

The unity of this paragraph would be destroyed by inserting a sentence that is not a part of the plan called for by the controlling idea. Try reading the paragraph with these sentences inserted between sentences 2 and 3: "People obviously have different biological rhythms. Some people go to bed early and awaken at 6:00 or 7:00 ready for a full day's work. Others cannot fall asleep before 12:00 or 1:00 a.m. and are not really prepared to face the workplace before 10:00 a.m." These three sentences, or even one of them, would shift the focus of the paragraph away from the controlling idea: *Flextime is here to stay.* To maintain unity in a paragraph, then, you must be conscious of your controlling idea each time you add a sentence.

Since the controlling idea gives direction to the other sentences in the paragraph, it usually appears early in the paragraph—as the first or second sentence. But it may be placed at the end of the paragraph if the writer wishes to build up to a dramatic closing.

31b Link the sentences in the paragraph so that the thought flows smoothly from one sentence to the next.

A coherent paragraph is one in which the relationship of any given sentence to the sentence before or after it is clear and the transitions between the sentences are smooth. A coherent paragraph is easy to read because there are no jarring breaks—the sentences are arranged in a clear, logical order (for example, by time; from general to specific; from least important to most important; or by location of items being described); and there are smooth transitions between sentences: (1) pronouns are used to refer to antecedents in preceding sentences; (2) words or ideas are repeated; (3) transitional expressions are used; and (4) sentence structure is made parallel.

The following paragraph illustrates the four methods of achieving coherence. The sentences are arranged in order of climax (from least important to most important); the methods of making smooth transitions between sentences are identified by numbers—1 through 4—that correspond to those cited above.

> There is much evidence that the roles of the sexes are changing. [3] First, and most noticeable, is the change in dress and appearance. Today many young men and women look alike. [1] Their hair may be similar in style. [1, 4] They may wear the same shirts and pants. [1, 4] They may in fact go to the same unisex hair stylists and boutiques. [3, 2] But more significant evidence of the shift in sex roles is apparent in the job market. While a generation ago no more than one out of ten women with young children was employed outside the home, today one out of three is working away from the home. [3] And positions that were once considered appropriate only for men are now being filled by women. [3, 2] Conversely, many men today are training to be nurses, secretaries, and flight attendants—positions once considered unmistakably feminine. [3, 2]

31c Develop ideas adequately so that each paragraph presents enough information about the controlling idea to satisfy the reader.

The length of a paragraph varies with its purpose. Thus a one-sentence paragraph or even a one-word paragraph ("Yes" or "No") may say emphatically all that the writer needs to say. Paragraphs that report dialogue are usually short because a new paragraph must begin each time the speaker changes. Most paragraphs in expository writing tend to vary in length from about seventy-five to two hundred fifty words, the average length being about one hundred words. And remember that when you write in longhand your paragraph looks much longer than it would if it were typed or set in print.

The controlling idea of a paragraph may be developed in a number of ways. Most experienced writers use several methods of development in each paragraph without having to think about what they are doing. But as an inexperienced writer, you may need to practice consciously the methods discussed below until you are able to use them automatically and naturally. A study of these methods will help you not only to think of things to say but also to organize your thoughts, since the method of development usually suggests a pattern of arrangement for the sentences in the paragraph.

(1) Use relevant details to develop the controlling idea.

The use of details is the most common method of developing a controlling idea, and almost every paragraph makes some use of it. Pertinent facts and details about the changing roles of the sexes are used to develop the controlling idea of the paragraph illustrating coherence. Notice that the most significant fact is discussed last, a common type of arrangement for this method of development.

(2) Use several closely related examples or one striking example to illustrate the controlling idea.

A paragraph developed by examples is almost certain to hold the reader's attention. The success of one of the most popular books ever printed, Dale Carnegie's *How to Win Friends and Influence People*, depends primarily on the author's use of hundreds of examples. Because of the interest generated by a well-chosen example, many essays and speeches begin with this type of development, like the following first paragraph from an essay about the workaholic.

> [1] When it comes to choosing between business and social activities, Howard Bronson knows where his priorities lie: with his job. [2] Bronson, who heads his own financial public relations firm, is up by four a.m. and has mapped out his day by the time he gets to his Manhattan office at 6:45. [3] He works at a furious pace, often skipping lunch, until about 6:30 in the evening. [4] Then, after dinner, he puts in another hour and a half of reading before turning in at 12:15.
>
> —"Thank God, It's Monday," *Dun's Review*, June 1980

Examples may be fully developed, like the one above, or simply listed in passing, like the series of examples in the following paragraph used to illustrate the characteristics of workaholics during childhood.

> [1] Marilyn Machlowitz, a psychologist for New York Life Insurance Co., has spent the past eight years studying the obsessive worker—first for her doctoral dissertation at Yale, more recently for her book *Workaholics: Living With Them, Working With Them*. [2] From interviews with 165 apparent workaholics, she has found that most exhibit identical characteristics early in their lives. [3] They turn games into imitations of work and go about them with intensity. [4] They set up lemonade stands, run sidewalk carnivals and cash in returnable soda bottles. Later, they sell more Girl Scout cookies, Christmas cards and magazine subscriptions than anyone else on the block. [5] And their teachers love them because they are such hard-working, attentive students.
>
> —"Thank God, It's Monday," *Dun's Review*, June 1980

(3) Use an extended definition to develop the controlling idea.

Sometimes a writer wants to explain a term more fully or more subjectively than it is defined in the dictionary. In that case the writer may compose a paragraph or even an entire essay to define a difficult term or a term that the writer wants the reader to perceive in a special way. Notice that the essayist Jon Stewart uses two paragraphs to define a silicon chip for a general audience of readers who may be unfamiliar with the workings of microprocessors and computers.

[1] The revolution, of course, is that wrought by the silicon chip, that virtually invisible, spiderlike network of tiny electronic circuits etched on a flake of silicon (sand) less than half the size of the fingertip. [2] In the form of microprocessors, or miniature computers, it is invading every aspect of American life—the way we play, work, even think.

[3] This computer-on-a-chip, with amazing powers of memory and computation, has immediate applications almost everywhere from universities to automobile engines, from corporate offices to farms, from hospitals to satellites. [4] Virtually any routine work can be taken over by the devices, which have shrunk to less than 1/30,000 the size of their original predecessors, those giant room-size computers of yesterday. [5] And they grow smaller and more versatile almost daily. IBM recently announced that it can now produce a chip containing 256,000 bits of information, four times as many as are crammed onto the most highly integrated chip today.

—Jon Stewart, "Computer Shock: The Inhuman Office of the Future,"
Saturday Review, June 23, 1979

(4) Use classification to develop the controlling idea.

Classification may be used to divide a key term in the controlling idea into categories. For example, the term "alternate work schedules" may be broken down into compressed time, flextime, part-time, and shared time. (See the plan for the following paragraph on p. 283.)

[1] Alternate work schedules are rapidly replacing the rigid eight- or nine-to-five workdays of the past. [2] For example, the 10-hour, four-day workweek has been used in industry for many years. [3] This type of compressed-time job schedule allows the worker to enjoy a regular three-day weekend. [4] But surpassing compressed-time scheduling in popularity with workers is flextime, which lets them choose their own hours to begin and end their workdays so long as they work a certain number of hours a week and so long as they are on the job during a mid-day core period. [5] Also, part-time work, which involves one out of every six workers in this country, continues to gain in popularity as people, especially the young, begin to value leisure as much as they do money. [6] And shared-time work schedules, whereby two employees share one full-time position, are saving employers as well as employees from massive lay-offs in an increasingly automated society.

(5) Use comparison or contrast to develop the controlling idea.

In everyday conversation people are continually explaining or evaluating something by comparing or contrasting it with something else. In compositions, too, comparison or contrast is often used. In general, the people, ideas, or objects to be compared or contrasted should belong to the same class (one type of room-mate is compared or contrasted with another type of roommate, not with some other type of person).

The following paragraph compares the importance of three values—work, family, and leisure—to people in today's society.

> [1] Along with family life, work and leisure always compete for people's time and allegiance. [2] One or the other is usually the center of gravity; rarely does the individual strike an equal balance among all three. [3] For the New Breed, family and work have grown less important and leisure more important. [4] When work and leisure are com-pared as sources of satisfaction in our surveys, only one out of five people (21 percent) states that work means more to them than leisure. [5] The majority (60 percent) say that while they enjoy their work, it is not their major source of satisfaction. [6] (The other 19 percent are so exhausted by the demands work makes of them that they cannot con-ceive of it as even a minor source of satisfaction.)
>
> —Daniel Yankelovich, "The New Psychological Contracts at Work,"
> *Psychology Today*, May 1978

(6) Use cause or effect to develop the controlling idea.

A paragraph that is developed by cause or effect describes the reasons why a par-ticular outcome has occurred. To use this method effectively, you must supply enough proof to convince your reader that you understand the cause or causes for a particular effect. The following two paragraphs rely primarily on comments made during interviews to persuade us that the editors of *Newsweek* have cor-rectly identified two causes for the American worker's lack of commitment to the work ethic.

> [1] The problem traces to two main factors: a younger work force—25 per cent of which is under 25 years old—and the nature of work itself in a highly industrialized society. [2] "It's mainly a problem of this younger worker," said Benjamin Aaron, direc-tor of the Institute of Industrial Relations at UCLA. [3] "He doesn't want to work to get ahead; he wants to work to get enough money for a while and then he wants to drop out." [4] Or, as Jerry Wurf, president of the American Federation of State, County and Municipal Employees, put it: "The Depression is something they learned about in a history class."
>
> [5] Once on the job, workers all too often find that, however good their wages and working conditions, work is a totally unsatisfying experience. [6] "People my age don't take much pride in this work," says Victoria Bowker, a 27-year-old blueprinter at Lockheed Aircraft. [7] "In the old days, you used to start a job and you used to finish it. [8] Now things have become so diversified you can't see your product; you start something and it goes through 50 million other hands before it's completed." [9] Mike Eckert, a longtime Lockheed employee twice Miss Bowker's age, agrees that things have changed. [10] "Today's management doesn't have any compassion for the person that's down the line," he says. [11] "They treat you like a machine . . . and you can't treat human nature that way." [12] And when a worker begins feeling like a machine, he'll probably resort to one of two alternatives: goldbrick, or start looking for another job. [13] "I'll tell you how attitudes are," UAW vice president Ken Bannon summed up last week. [14] "You will find people who say they would rather work in cleanup and take a

cut of 15 cents an hour than work the assembly line. [15] At least on cleanup you have the choice of sweeping the pile in the corner or sweeping the pile by the post."

—"Too Many U.S. Workers No Longer Give a Damn,"
Newsweek, April 24, 1972

(7) Use a combination of methods to develop the controlling idea.

The various methods of developing a controlling idea have been listed and il-lustrated separately, but almost every paragraph makes use of more than one method. For example, the paragraph developed by cause or effect [see (**6**) above] also uses details, and the paragraph developed by classification [see (**4**)] also uses definition and examples to explain the types of alternate work schedules given.

31d Make a simple plan for your paragraph.

Since paragraphs do not often include more than twelve sentences, you do not need a detailed or complicated outline to follow. But most writers jot down their controlling ideas and main points of development before they begin to write their paragraphs. Even a simple plan helps writers to evaluate two qualities of their projected paragraphs: unity and development. If writers cannot clearly relate a point of development to the controlling idea, the item can be deleted in the plan-ning stage. If writers can think of only one or two points of development, they know that they must either find other points before they can compose the paragraph or write another controlling idea that they can better substantiate.

On the next page is the plan for the paragraph developed by classification (**4**). Notice that the writer, after jotting down a number of points, crossed out those that do not develop the controlling idea or that would expand one point so much that the focus of the paragraph would be lost. Also notice that the writer chose to change the order of the four divisions sometime during the planning stage.

Simple Plan for Paragraph Developed by Classification

Controlling idea: Alternate work schedules
are rapidly replacing the rigid
eight— or nine-to-five workdays
of the past.

Development

II. 1. flextime
2. choice of when to start and finish working
3. ~~suitable to biological rhythms~~
4. work a core period of hours

I. 5. compressed time
6. 10-hour, four-day workweek
7. ~~10/70 with seven days off~~
8. weekends extended
9. long used by industry

III. 10. part-time
11. ~~friend of mine who worked part time at two jobs~~
12. much more leisure time
13. suits changing values
14. one out of every six workers

IV. 15. shared time
16. full-time position split
17. ~~two five-hour shifts~~
18. ~~no overtime pay necessary~~
19. helps to prevent lay-offs
20. ~~many employees asked for shared time to continue education~~

Analyzing paragraphs   Exercise 31–1

NAME _____ SCORE _____

DIRECTIONS   Analyze the unity, coherence, and development of the following paragraph by answering the questions that follow it. When the question asks, "*Which sentence . . . ?*" use the sentence's number to identify your answer.

¹During the 1970s and 1980s both men and women register complaints about the role of women in the work force. ²A study conducted by the Department of Labor reveals that half the married women who work full time would prefer part-time employment. ³Obviously, a possible reason for women's unhappiness with their jobs is revealed by their salaries: women generally earn far less than men for the same kind of work. ⁴Some employers feel that women should earn less than men. ⁵They point out that women are less dependable at work than men. ⁶And they claim that women are absent from work more frequently than men. ⁷Finally, these employers feel that women are temperamentally unsuited for management or higher-paying positions. ⁸In a survey conducted by the *Harvard Business Review*, more than half of the executives interviewed insisted that women did not make good supervisors. ⁹Although everyone agrees that the role of women in the labor force is much improved over what it was a hundred years ago, clearly many individuals of both sexes are still unhappy with the lot of the working woman, albeit for different reasons.

1. Which sentence states the controlling idea of the paragraph?_____

2. What is the major method of development used in the paragraph?

    _____

3. Which sentences show the use of comparison or contrast? _____

4. What is the key term that is repeated throughout the paragraph?

    _____

5. Which sentences use transitional expressions? _____

6. Which two sentences are linked by parallel structure? _____

7. Which sentence is the shortest one in the paragraph? _____

   What is its purpose? _____

8. Which sentence is the clincher, the one that repeats the controlling idea?

   (Not all paragraphs have this kind of sentence.) _____

9. What is the basis for the arrangement of the sentences in the paragraph: is it

   by time, from general to specific, by order of climax, or by location of what is

   being described? _____

10. Which two sentences use an introductory phrase to vary from the usual word

    order of placing the subject first? _____

    Which sentences begin with a single adverb? _____

    Which sentence uses an introductory subordinate clause? _____

The controlling idea and the methods of development

NAME _____

DIRECTIONS   For each of the following four paragraphs list (1) the number of the sentence that states the controlling idea; (2) the main method of development used to support the controlling idea; and (3) an additional method of development used in the paragraph.

PARAGRAPH ONE

[1]Of course, not everyone who works long hours is a workaholic. [2]Many people simply have more work than they can handle on a normal schedule. [3]Others work for companies where long hours are part of the job. [4]Some Wall Street law firms, for example, are notorious for expecting associates to work late into the night; and young lawyers, even when they have no work to do, frequently remain at their desks until their superiors have left the office. [5]There are also a number of people who reluctantly moonlight because they need the money.

—"Thank God, It's Monday," *Dun's Review*, June 1980

1. Controlling idea _____

2. Main method of development _____

3. Additional method of development _____

PARAGRAPH TWO

[1]Psychologists are also starting to unravel the mystery of why some people turn out to be workaholics while others do not. [2]It is becoming increasingly apparent that the process begins in early childhood. [3]Psychiatrist Lawrence Susser, who treats workaholics on his yacht in New Rochelle, New York, claims that workaholics are the products of "controlling parents"; that is, parents who, rather than simply supporting or setting guidelines for their children, are constantly pushing them to excel. [4]The children fear that unless they live up to these expectations, love will be withheld. [5]Eventually they develop a sort of "inner

voice" that prods them in the same manner as their parents did. [6] This voice can be very demanding, Dr. Susser says. [7] It does not let them relax.

—"Thank God, It's Monday," *Dun's Review*, June 1980

1. Controlling idea _____

2. Main method of development _____

3. Additional method of development _____

PARAGRAPH THREE

[1] Many people mistakenly think that creativity is the ability to think thoughts that no one else has ever thought. [2] In fact, creativity is just a way of looking at the ordinary in a different way. [3] Alex Osborn, one of the pioneers in the study of creativity and imagination, discovered that almost everyone is more creative than he thinks. [4] We usually don't recognize our good ideas as creativity in action. [5] For example, in a large midwestern city a gang of thieves had worked out a coordinated routine that was so smooth and fast that they could break into a clothing store, sweep the clothes off the racks, and be gone before the police could answer the alarm. [6] Then a young detective got an idea. [7] He asked all the clothing merchants in the area to alternate the way they placed the hangers on the rack. [8] He told the store owners: "Turn one hook toward the wall and the next one toward the aisle. [9] Do it that way throughout the store." [10] When police answered the next alarm they found the frustrated thieves removing the garments one at a time. [11] Everyday "shirtsleeve creativity" is simply the adaptation of existing ideas—taking another look at all of the pieces of the situation from a new perspective.

—Dale O. Ferrier, "Shirtsleeve Creativity,"
The Rotarian, July 1981

The controlling idea and the methods of development

1. Controlling idea _____

2. Main method of development _____

3. Additional method of development _____

PARAGRAPH FOUR

[1] Even in the past decade, the average U.S. farm worker's productivity has increased 185 percent, while the manufacturing worker has upped productivity by 90 percent. [2] Those figures may not be as high as in the past, or in other parts of the world today, but they certainly compare favorably with the performance of U.S. office workers. [3] In the past 10 years, according to studies done by the Massachusetts Institute of Technology and others, the white-collar worker's productivity has increased a mere four percent. [4] This figure is reached by measuring time spent on work tasks, as well as by counting units (letters typed, reports written, cases handled) where possible. [5] Four percent is the total for the whole past 10 years, not an annual rate of productivity increase.

—Raymond P. Kurshan, "White-collar Productivity,"

The Rotarian, June 1981

1. Controlling idea _____

2. Main method of development _____

3. Additional method of development _____

Mastering paragraphs: a review

NAME _____

DIRECTIONS   A paragraph requires planning if it is to have unity and if it is to develop the controlling idea fully. For a paragraph about work, make notes for a controlling idea and the supporting development. (You may find the facts and ideas presented in the exercises of this workbook useful in planning your paragraph.) Once you have made your list, look it over carefully to make sure that all the points of development clearly support your controlling idea. Then arrange the points in a logical order. Finally, write your paragraph, using your controlling idea in the first or second sentence.

SUGGESTED SUBJECTS

1. the advantages of working part time
2. the best (or worst) use of leisure time
3. plans for your leisure time
4. the reasons why people work (or why you work)
5. proof that people in our society value work too much (or too little)
6. the types of jobs available in the field of your major
7. the reasons why you have chosen a particular major or career
8. the types of writing demanded by your chosen profession
9. the advantages and/or disadvantages of early retirement or of "stopping out" (temporarily leaving school)
10. the effects of automation on the job market or on your chosen profession

CONTROLLING IDEA

DEVELOPMENT

PARAGRAPH

PARAGRAPH (CONTINUED)

32

Learn to write a unified and coherent composition in which the thesis statement is adequately developed.

The elements that are most important in writing the composition—unity, coherence, and adequate development—are the same ones that are crucial in the paragraph. But the composition's greater length calls for more careful planning than is demanded by the paragraph. And the composition, unlike most individual paragraphs, has a title, an introduction, and a conclusion.

32a Choose an appropriate topic and limit it properly.

The appropriateness of a topic depends on the writer, the reader, and the occasion. You must know and care enough about the topic to have something interesting to say. But you must also be sure that the topic is acceptable to your intended reader or readers and suitable to the occasion on which it will be read.

How well you limit the topic depends on your ability to focus on an aspect that you can cover adequately in the time allotted to the writing of the paper. For example, "occupational writing" is a topic that might be covered in a book; it is clearly not limited enough to be discussed adequately in the hour or two most students have for writing an in-class paper. There are several methods of limiting a general topic.

(1) Brainstorm the topic.

Spend five or ten minutes writing down everything you can think of about the subject. Then, from the list, choose one item that seems sufficiently narrowed down for your purpose. You may then need to brainstorm the item you have chosen to provide the development for your topic.

(2) Ask yourself the standard reporter's questions about the topic: "Who?" "What?" "How?" "Why?" "When?" "Where?"

(3) Make a simple outline of the broad topic and choose an idea from one of the Roman-numeral headings as your limited topic. (See also **32b**.)

(4) Let the purpose of the composition help you limit the topic.

You might write a composition to inform the reader about the facts of the topic (expository essay); to argue some point about the topic (persuasive essay); to retell in chronological order the events relevant to the topic (narrative essay); or to describe the appearance—sight, sounds, smells, and so on—of the topic (descriptive essay).

32b Make a working plan, or an outline, for the composition.

The most important part of the outline is the thesis statement, a simple or complex sentence that states clearly and exactly the focus of your essay. The thesis statement corresponds to the controlling ideas of the paragraphs: it determines or directs the controlling idea found in each paragraph of the composition.

Roman numerals mark the headings that set forth the main points used to develop the thesis statement. The subheadings (signaled by capital letters) present the specific proof for the main headings. If the composition is very long—ten or more pages—further subheadings (signaled by Arabic numbers and then by lower-case letters) may come under the capital-letter divisions.

The outline may or may not have an introduction and a conclusion. If during the planning stage you have in mind a way to introduce your thesis statement, write it down as a part of the outline. Likewise, if an idea for a conclusion or a concluding sentence occurs to you while planning the outline, record it at the time.

SENTENCE OUTLINE

How Not to Choose a Career

Introduction: The choice of a career is one of the most important decisions a person makes in life. Yet many people are poorly prepared for this decision.

Thesis: Students have four major misconceptions about how to choose a career.

I. They think they must make the decision unaided.

    A. Qualified friends and family members can be helpful.

    B. High-school and college counselors have special training to guide students in selecting their careers.

    C. Employment agencies can help students find the jobs that fit their skills and talents.

II. They think that their decisions must be based entirely
on reason.

    A. Emotions are important in career planning.

    B. There are many examples of unhappy workers in
occupations that seemed to be logical choices.

III. They think that their decisions must never be changed.

    A. The changing job market often necessitates a
change in career plans.

    B. Actual work experience often reveals a wrong
decision.

IV. They think that their decision must make them
constantly happy.

    A. There is a good and a bad side to all decisions.

    B. Other aspects of life also influence happiness.

    C. In any job there is the likelihood of an
emotional setback.

Conclusion: If students are aware of these common
misconceptions about how to choose a career, they will
be better prepared for one of life's most important
decisions.

TOPIC OUTLINE

How Not to Choose a Career

Thesis: Students have four major misconceptions

about how to choose a career.

   I. That the decision must be made alone,

      without the help of others

      A. Qualified friends and family members

      B. High-school and college counselors

      C. Employment agencies

  II. That the decision must be based entirely

      on reason

      A. The importance of emotions in decision

         making

      B. Examples of unhappy workers in occupa-

         tions that seemed to be logical choices

 III. That the decisions must never be changed

      A. Changing job market

      B. Realization of a wrong choice

  IV. That the decision must make a person constantly

      happy

      A. The good and the bad side of all decisions

      B. The importance of other aspects of life

      C. The likelihood of emotional setbacks

Note these points about sentence and topic outlines:
(1) The thesis is stated as a sentence regardless of the type of outline.
(2) The introduction and the conclusion may or may not be included in the outline.
(3) In both the sentence and the topic outlines, there must be at least two headings at each level (two Roman numerals, two capital letters) for the development to be adequate.
(4) In the sentence outline, only sentences are used; in the topic outline, parallel structure is used.
(5) In any outline, proper indention is maintained to make the outline easy to read.

Avoid making these four errors in outlines:
(1) *Overlapping headings.* If information in one heading (for example, in II.B.) overlaps information in another (for example, in I.A.) or restates it in different words, then the essay will be repetitious.
(2) *Misarranged headings.* The headings show the order of presentation. If the arrangement is not logical, the paper cannot be coherent. (See also **31b**.)
(3) *Inadequately developed headings.* Usually three main headings (Roman numerals) and at least two subheadings (capital letters) are necessary to supply adequate development.
(4) *Needless shifts in tense or number.* This weakness is more noticeable in the sentence outline than in the topic outline. Usually a needless shift in the outline is carried over to the composition.

32c Write the first draft, using the outline as a guide.

An outline is a working plan; it is not a composition, complete with varied sentences and carefully selected words. It is a guide that shows the main ideas you intend to cover in the essay and the proof or development you have thought of for those ideas. It may be changed, added to, or subtracted from when you write the paper.

Although the sentence and the topic outlines do suggest where paragraph breaks will occur in the essay, there is no rule demanding that each paragraph cover a Roman-numeral heading or a capital-letter subheading. In a short essay the Roman-numeral headings usually indicate the paragraph divisions; in a longer essay the capital-letter subheadings do.

If your outline is well planned, your essay will be unified—that is, the reader will see the relationship of each paragraph to the thesis statement. The essay is coherent if each paragraph flows smoothly into the one that follows it. The reader should immediately see the relationship of a new paragraph, not only to the thesis, but also to the paragraph that precedes it. Coherence in an essay is achieved by the same methods used in a paragraph. (See **31b**.)

On page 298 is an example of the first page of a rough draft for a composition on "How Not to Choose a Career."

How Not to Choose a Career

As small children most of us easily find our careers in a row of buttons: doctor, lawyer, teacher, police officer, fire fighter, astronaut, dancer. Ten years or so later, when what we want to be in life is a real question, many of us continue to be arbitrary in our choice of careers. We may decide ~~be certain that we want to~~ be accountants even though we have never been good at mathematics, or we may choose to be nurses even though we cannot tolerate the sight of an open wound or an infected eye. ~~We sometimes make the most important decision of our lives without any reasonable guidelines.~~ It is not surprising to learn ~~then~~, that many of us, will be ~~are~~ unhappy with our work, for we have approach ~~approached~~ the choice of a career with a variety of misconceptions.

The first and perhaps most serious misconception ~~that~~ (many of us ~~have~~ think) about career choices is that we must make the decision alone, unaided. Actually there are many people who ~~not only want to help us make the decision but who~~ can also help us make the right decision: friends, family members, teachers, and guidance counselors.

32d Include an introduction and a conclusion in your composition.

In the average-length student paper—three hundred to five hundred words—the introduction and the conclusion need not be long, but they must be included. The introduction gets the reader interested in the body of the paper; the conclusion should wrap up the points you have made. The introduction need be no more than the thesis statement or a sentence that suggests the thesis statement. The conclusion may be no more than a restatement, in different words, of the thesis; or, if the thesis is only suggested in the introduction, it may be the first forthright statement of the thesis.

Most students find they have more time to write their introductions than their conclusions. They may use as an introduction a striking example, a shocking statement that is later explained, or a question that leads into the thesis. The writer strengthens the conclusion by suggesting a solution to the problem presented in the essay. In the conclusion the writer should never pose a new point that is not to be explored nor apologize to the reader. The writer should simply make the reader feel that the essay has ended, having accomplished what it set out to accomplish.

32e Give the composition a title and arrange the pages in order.

Usually a title will occur to you during the planning or the writing of the essay. Certainly you should not spend the time you need for writing the paper in sitting and thinking about a title. If you have not thought of a title by the time you finish the composition, use the topic or some form of it—for example, "Common Misconceptions About Career Choices."

When time permits, though, give attention to the title. Choose one that is provocative, that will make a reader want to read your essay. But never sacrifice appropriateness for cleverness; above all else, the title should suit the content of the essay. In general, it is best to avoid long, wordy titles or declarative-sentence titles that tell the reader too much about the essay.

Many instructors prefer the title on a separate page, along with your name, the course name and section number, the date, and the paper number. Remember that the title should not be punctuated with quotation marks or italics (underlining) unless you are referring to a literary or artistic work and that the title should be followed by an end mark of punctuation only if it is a question or an exclamation. (See also **8c.**) The sentence or topic outline follows the title page, and then comes the paper itself. Number the pages of your paper in the upper right-hand corner, using Arabic numbers, but do not place a number on page 1.

32f Proofread your paper carefully and make all necessary changes in spelling, punctuation, and phrasing. Then recopy or retype any pages on which you made a number of changes.

Here are six suggestions for proofreading that may help you to revise your composition:

(1) Wait at least one day, if possible, before you proofread your first draft. Then you will be more likely to spot weaknesses and mistakes.

(2) Proofread at least three times: once for organization; a second time, out loud, for style; and a third time for grammar, punctuation, and spelling. If you have serious problems with grammar, punctuation, or spelling, proofread still another time for the error or errors you most frequently make.

(3) When proofreading for errors, slow your reading down. To make yourself go more slowly, actually point to each word with your pencil as you read. If you have real difficulties with spelling, try reading each line from right to left instead of the usual left to right so that you will notice words individually.

(4) Read your writing assignment to someone else and ask your listener to stop you when something does not make sense or does not sound right.

(5) Type your written work. Even if you do not type well enough to make the final copy, type at least one draft of your work. Typing the manuscript forces you to take a close look at what you have written. (Many writers do most of their editing while they are typing.)

(6) Plan to spend more time revising your introduction than any other part of your paper. Your introduction is often the first thing you write, and it is usually the part of your paper most in need of rewriting.

The essay

NAME _____

DIRECTIONS   Choose a topic from the list of suggested subjects in Exercise **31–3** (p. 291) or a topic of your own for an essay of three hundred to five hundred words. (If you choose to write about work, you may find the facts and ideas presented in this workbook useful in planning your essay.) After making either a sentence or a topic outline below, write a first draft of the composition. Proofread it carefully, making any changes in grammar, punctuation, spelling, or style that seem necessary. Then recopy any pages that required more than five or six revisions. Finally, make a title page, following your instructor's directions, and number the pages of the paper, using Arabic numbers, beginning in the upper right-hand corner of page 2.

TOPIC

OUTLINE

OUTLINE (CONTINUED)

33

Learn to write the three main types of business composition: the letter, the memorandum, and the report.

Examples of the letter, the memorandum, and the report are given in this section to serve as a guide to the format and content expected by businesses.

33a Learn to write the most common types of business letters: the letter of application, the claim and adjustment letters, and the order letter.

Of the four letter styles used today, the most popular are the modified block style (illustrated in the letter of application) and the semiblock style (illustrated in the claim and adjustment letters and in the order letter).

LETTER OF APPLICATION: modified block style

56 Finley Street
Smithfield, NC 27512
June 12, 1982

Dr. Latimore Voss
Head of Radiology
Duke Hospital
Durham, NC 27606

Dear Dr. Voss:

**IDENTIFY POSITION
SOUGHT AND HOW
LEARNED ABOUT**

**INDICATE MAJOR
QUALIFICATIONS
FOR JOB**

I would like to apply for the position of
X-ray technician that you advertised in the
Durham Sun on June 8. I have just completed
an Associate of Applied Science Degree in
X-ray technology at Wake Technical Institute
and have worked for two summers as an assis-
tant to a professional X-ray technician, so
I feel I am qualified to fill the position.

**REFER TO
RÉSUMÉ**

As you will notice from my résumé, I have been
working in hospitals and doctors' offices since
my junior year in high school. From this experience I have become familiar with routine office
procedures and with many of the business forms
that are used in a variety of medical fields.

**REQUEST
INTERVIEW**

I am available to begin work immediately. Could
you suggest a time when you might interview me
for the position you advertised? I can be reached
at 672-3334 any weekday between noon and 6:00 P.M.

Yours sincerely,

Calvin Atwood

Calvin Atwood

Enclosure

RÉSUMÉ

CALVIN ATWOOD

56 Finley Street
Smithfield, NC 27512
(919) 672-3334

Personal data   Date of birth: April 4, 1961
Marital status: single
Health: excellent

GIVE
EDUCATION
IN REVERSE
CHRONOLOGICAL
ORDER

Education   WAKE TECHNICAL INSTITUTE
Raleigh, NC 27603

Associate of Applied
Science Degree, 1982

Major courses: life sciences,
radiological procedures, radiological technology, clinical
education, radiobiology

USE PHRASES,
NOT SENTENCES

Background courses: report
writing, radiographic quality
assurance, introduction to epi-
demiology, general psychology

SMITHFIELD HIGH SCHOOL
Smithfield, NC 27512

Graduated in 1979 in upper quarter
of class

Extracurricular activities:
Beta Club, Student Council,
baseball team, school newspaper,
president of Allied Health Club

GIVE
EXPERIENCE
IN REVERSE
CHRONOLOGICAL
ORDER

Experience   1979-82: assistant to Mr. Cleve
Ogburn, Wake County Health Clinic

1977-79: worked summers in
Dr. Paul Godfrey's office in
Smithfield and at the Smithfield
Health Clinic

References   Dr. Lester Owens. Head of Radiology
Wake Technical Institute
Raleigh, NC 27603

Mr. Cleve Ogburn, Director
Wake County Health Clinic
Raleigh, NC 27510

Dr. Paul Godfrey
164 Jones Street
Smithfield, NC 27512

CLAIM AND ADJUSTMENT LETTERS: semiblock style

50 Locust Street
Neva, PA 19133
April 10, 1982

Quality Assurance Manager
Superb Coffee-Makers
Box G
Newark, NJ 10500

Dear Sir or Madam:

IDENTIFY
THE TRANSACTION

     I am returning by United Parcel the automatic coffee-maker I purchased for $35.95 plus $1.44 sales tax on December 6, 1981, from the May Company in Allentown, Pennsylvania. I mailed the warranty

EXPLAIN
THE PROBLEM

card to you on December 10. The coffee-maker leaks one-half to a full cup of water during the brewing process.

EXPLAIN WHAT
YOU WANT DONE

     Will you please promptly replace or repair the coffee-maker or return my purchase price?

Yours truly,

Catherine Bush

Ms. Catherine Bush

Box G
Newark, NJ 10500
April 24, 1982

Ms. Catherine Bush
50 Locust Street
Neva, PA 19133

Dear Ms. Bush:

**IDENTIFY
THE COMPLAINT**

We are sorry that you have had difficulty with our automatic coffee-maker. We have sent your coffee-maker to our Service Department for

**EXPLAIN WHAT
ACTION IS
BEING TAKEN**

your area, located in Allentown, Pennsylvania, at 210 Broad Street. You should hear from our service representative within the next few weeks.

Sincerely yours,

Roberta Juliana

Roberta Juliana
Quality Assurance Manager
Superb Coffee-Makers

RJ: drw

ORDER LETTER: semiblock style

88 Fourth Street
Fresno, CA 77406
September 24, 1982

The Woodshed
15 Juniper Street
Dearborn, MA 01730

Ladies and Gentlemen:

IDENTIFY
THE ITEM
WANTED

    Please send me the coat tree, item number CT-103, advertised in your fall catalog for $49.95. I would like the coat tree in a dark stain.

EXPLAIN
METHOD OF
PAYMENT

    Enclosed is my certified check for $59.95 to cover the cost and the shipping charges ($10.00).

BE COURTEOUS

    Thank you in advance for your service.

Sincerely yours,

Laurence Ancel

Lawrence Ancel

Enclosure
certified check, $59.95

Business letters

NAME _____

DIRECTIONS   Using the modified or the semiblock style, write a letter of application for a job in your field, a letter of complaint about a product you bought that is not performing satisfactorily, and a letter ordering a product that you would like to purchase by mail (use a catalog advertisement or the "For Sale" column of a newspaper or magazine for the product information). Do your planning of the letter in the space provided below, but type or neatly handwrite your letters on white bond paper.

PLANNING SPACE

PLANNING SPACE (CONTINUED)

33b Study the procedure for writing an interoffice memorandum.

Many offices have their own preprinted forms for interoffice memorandums. The forms are used to communicate various kinds of information within a company: confirmation of a conversation, clarification of previous correspondence, requests, congratulations, and announcements.

REQUEST MEMORANDUM

TO   Greg Carlson
_____

FROM   Donna Wayne
_____

SUBJECT Triangle employment figures
_____

DATE   10 June 1982
_____

    Greg, before my meeting with the president of Triangle Corporation I will need to have the employment figures for 1981: the number of females and the number of males hired; the number of females and the number of males fired or laid off; the number of employees who retired or who required disability leave; and the total number of employees on the payroll at the end of 1981.

    Can you please furnish me with these figures by June 17?

33c Learn to write a report.

Businesses require reports for a variety of purposes: to describe mechanisms and processes; to provide instructions; to relate progress on the development of products or procedures; to analyze systems and procedures; to present proposals; and to record trips, minutes of meetings, and accidents. Most of these types of reports have been discussed in the exercise material of this workbook.

(1) Learn to write a process analysis.

Most reports that you are likely to write will be developed by process analysis, a step-by-step explanation of how something is made, how it works, or how it is done. You may practice this kind of report by writing a process analysis of something you are familiar with. What follows is a process analysis of how a thermometer works.

```
                      How a Thermometer Works


        There is no instrument the American home depends

   on more than the thermometer.  On a winter day, for

   example, the thermometer tells us how cold it is out-

   side or how warm inside, whether or not we have a fever from

   our winter cold, when the roast in our oven is done, and

   if the chocolate mixture on the stove has reached the

   soft-ball stage.  Whether it is a thermometer out-

   side our door, a thermostat on our furnace, or a

   thermometer in our mouth, our meat, or our candy, the

   same process is at work to show us how hot or cold

   something is.

        A thermometer is usually a glass tube with a small

   bulb at the end.  The bulb contains a liquid, either

   mercury or alcohol, that rises or falls inside the glass

   tube.  The tube has degree markings that show how much

   the liquid has risen or fallen:  the higher the liquid
```

rises, the hotter the solid, liquid, or gas we are measuring; the lower the liquid falls, the colder the solid, liquid, or gas. The exact temperature is determined by noting the degree marking that is even with the top of the liquid.

The process that causes the liquid inside the tube to rise or fall is quite simple. When what is being measured is hotter than the liquid inside the tube, the liquid expands, or swells up. Since there is not enough room inside the bulb of the thermometer for all of the expanding liquid, some of the liquid rises in the glass tube. The liquid stops rising when its temperature becomes the same as that of the solid, liquid, or gas being measured. The opposite movement occurs when something colder than the liquid in the bulb of the thermometer is being measured. The liquid contracts, or shrinks, and some of it falls down the tube into the bulb. The liquid continues to go back into the bulb until its temperature becomes the same as that of the solid, liquid, or gas being measured. Because exterior temperatures can be very cold, alcohol--which will not freeze until the temperature drops to 170 degrees below zero--is used as the liquid in an outdoor thermometer. For an indoor thermometer, mercury is most commonly used.

The temperature shown on the glass tube may be measured in either Farenheit or Celsius degrees. The scale for both is based on the temperature at which water boils and freezes. On a Farenheit scale--the kind

used largely in the United States--water boils at 212

degrees and freezes at 32 degrees; on a Celsius scale,

water boils at 100 degrees and freezes at 0 degrees.

In 1975 the United States Congress voted for

voluntary conversion to the Celsius scale to make

our system of measurement consistent with that used

in most of the world. At the present time many ther-

mometers show both Farenheit and Celsius degrees to

help us grow accustomed to the new system. Whatever

scale is used, people simply cannot do without ther-

mometers, because so many of our everyday activities

depend on measurement of temperature.

The report   Exercise 33-2

NAME _____

DIRECTIONS   Write a process analysis report in which you explain clearly and fully how something is made (for example, pizza, honey, or soap), how something is done (for example, registration at college, tuning-up an automobile engine, or learning to ski), or how something works (for example, the heart, a camera, or a solar heating system).

In the first paragraph introduce your process to the reader by identifying its purpose and significance. In the body of the report, describe in detail each of the steps in the operation of the process, using headings if the steps are lengthy or complex. In the conclusion, summarize the steps if the process is a complex one and/or make any additional comments to remind your readers of your introduction and so prepare them for the ending of the report.

PLANNING SPACE

PLANNING SPACE (CONTINUED)

(2) Learn to write a documented report.

Some reports that you may be asked to prepare will be based on research—on various experts' findings or speculations about a given topic. The use of facts and ideas gathered from sources requires an ability to do three things in addition to the usual planning, writing, and proofreading needed for any piece of composition: (1) paraphrase material taken from sources—that is, you must be able to report clearly and accurately in your own words the ideas and facts that someone else has presented; (2) quote exactly any series of three or more words that you decide to take verbatim from a source; and (3) provide documentation for the facts and ideas that you take from sources (the form of documentation varies depending on what guide you are following; the important thing is to follow exactly the format you are asked to use in documenting your research).

What follows is a documented report about the types of work schedules predicted for the year 2000. The source material for the first three notes is presented on page 320 so that you can see how the writer has handled both paraphrasing and direct quotations. The notes, which are included at the end of the report, and the bibliography entries follow the format of one popular guide for documentation—the style sheet of the Modern Language Association. Notice that the report has headings for the various divisions of the discussion, a common practice for a piece of business or technical writing that is more than two pages long.

No More Nine to Five: The Work Schedules of the Future

Andrew Varner

English 101, Section 55

Mr. Koessler

May 6, 1982

Outline

Thesis: Four main alternatives to the nine-to-five workday

seem destined to replace rigid time schedules.

I. Flextime

A. Definition of

B. Advantages of

C. History of

D. Reactions to

II. Part-time

A. Amount of

B. Reasons for spread

C. Companies' need for

III. Shared time

A. Definition of

B. Benefits to companies

C. Benefits to employees

D. Use of in California

IV. Nighttime

A. Increases in

B. Advantages of

V. Evidence of new schedules

A. All-night supermarkets

B. All-night banking

C. All-night entertainment

D. Traffic patterns

SAMPLE SOURCE MATERIAL

FOR NOTE 1

"Once we understand this, it comes as no surprise that one of the fastest-spreading innovations in industry during the 1970's was 'flextime'—an arrangement that permits workers, within predetermined limits, to choose their own working hours. Instead of requiring everyone to arrive at the factory gate or the office at the same time, or even at pre-fixed staggered times, the company operating on flextime typically sets certain core hours when everyone is expected to show up, and specifies other hours as flexible. Each employee may choose which of the flexible hours he or she wishes to spend working."

—Alvin Toffler, *The Third Wave*

FOR NOTE 2

"A typical flextime arrangement allows employees to put in their eight hours anytime within, for example, a 12-hour period, providing they work a mandatory 'core period' that provides midday stability."

—Jonathan Wolman, "Work Place 2000"

FOR NOTE 3

"This means that a 'day person'—a person whose biological rhythms routinely awaken him or her early in the morning—can choose to arrive at work at, say, 8:00 A.M., while a 'night person,' whose metabolism is different, can choose to start working at 10:00 or 10:30 A.M. It means that an employee can take time off for household chores, or to shop, or to take a child to the doctor. Groups of workers who wish to go bowling together early in the morning or late in the afternoon can jointly set their schedules to make it possible."

—Alvin Toffler, *The Third Wave*

No More Nine to Five: The Work Schedules of the Future

In a popular song of the 1980s Dolly Parton bemoans the
work schedule of many an American employee: "Working nine
to five--What a way to make a living." But if present
trends continue, it may well be that few workers by the year
2000 will need to complain about the nine-to-five syn-
drome. During the 1960s many variations from the nine-to-
five work schedules appeared which have become popular during
the 1970s and 1980s. These variations--flextime, part-
time, shared time, and nighttime--may well become standard
operating procedures in the near future.

Flextime

Alvin Toffler, in his best-seller about life in the
1980s, The Third Wave, describes flextime as "an arrangement that permits workers, within predetermined limits, to
choose their own working hours." Although there may be a
set number of core hours when all employees are expected to
work--say, for example, from 10:00 until 2:00--the remain-
ing three or four hours of the employee's day may be completed whenever the worker chooses.[1] The "core
period"--from 10:00 to 2:00--insures employers of a stable

midday staff[2] while the flexible schedule for the rest of
the day gives employees the freedom to plan their days to
accommodate their own and their families' needs. Even more
important, perhaps, workers can schedule their jobs around
their biological rhythms: people who awaken early can
report to work by 8:00 while those who stay up late and so
awaken late can start working at 10:00.[3] One final advantage of flextime for all society is the improvement in traffic patterns provided by different starting and finishing
times for workers.[4]

Flextime, which was introduced into West Germany in
1965 as a way to make the job market more appealing to women
with small children, was so successful that within two years
all 12,000 of the employees of a German aircraft company ex-
perimenting with it were using flextime schedules. Flextime
spread rapidly throughout other European nations as well as
in Great Britain. Then during the 1970s multinational
firms, like Nestlé and Lufthansa, exported flextime to the
United States. In a few short years after its introduction
in this country 13 percent of all United States companies
were making some use of flextime scheduling.[5]

Surveys, like one conducted by Psychology Today in
1978, suggest that the American worker strongly approves of
flextime; fully 78 percent of those questioned by Psychology Today wanted to have some say in the time they started
and finished their workday.[6] Employers, while they
acknowledge some problems with individualized work

schedules, seem equally satisfied with the system; as proof, only two percent of the companies that have tried flextime have returned to conventional schedules.[7] Based, then, on present trends, flextime seems certain to replace the rigid work schedules that people have followed since the outset of the Industrial Revolution. Looking ahead to the workplace in the year 2001, William Abbott, editor of the World Future Society's newsletter, Careers Tomorrow, says quite confidently, "Workers will schedule their own hours under flextime."[8]

Part-time

Just as remarkable a variation from rigid work schedules as flextime is the part-time movement that has swept the country during the past twenty years. In 1977 the economist Eli Ginzburg pointed out that 30 percent of all the work in this country was being done by part-time workers.[9] Alvin Toffler summarizes the increase in the number of part-time workers in this way: "In all, there is now one part-time worker for every five full-timers in the United States, and the part-time work force has been growing twice as fast as the full-time force since 1954." Indeed part-time employment has proved so popular with workers that researchers at Georgetown University have predicted almost all jobs in the future will be performed by part-time workers.[10]

Part-time work has flourished during the last twenty years for a number of reasons. Perhaps most important has been the growing number of working mothers in the job force who need to increase the family's income but who do not want to be separated from their children for the entire day. Part-time work also appeals to the elderly, who have retired from full-time work, and to students and the handicapped, who often cannot work a full eight-hour day.[11] In addition, there are many people today who simply choose part-time work because it gives them the free time they need to explore other goals--like a hobby, a sport, art, or education. "We are in the midst of a Value Revolution," according to William Abbott. "For many people, the acquisition of material symbols no longer is the primary goal in life."[12] Such people will settle for the decrease in pay that comes with part-time work to satisfy their other ambitions.[13]

Part-time work has become popular with employers because of the high incidence of absenteeism among workers. For example, in automobile plants, where a high percentage of workers invariably have an ailment dubbed "the Friday flu," employers have resorted to hiring part-time workers to fill in. A benefit offered by many companies today--the sabbatical--also causes employers to seek part-timers for the absent workers' positions. Steelworkers today have a 13-week sabbatical every seven years as part of their contract; the Rolm Corporation has gone a step further and permits employees with six years of service to periodically

take time off with pay. Part-time workers are also needed
to fill the spaces left by vacationing employees. The
United Auto Workers claim that each day there are 2,368 Ford
workers on a personal holiday.[14] In a variety of situations,
then, the part-time worker provides security for large companies that they can continue to function. As more and more
benefits--such as longer vacations, sabbaticals, and educational leaves--are provided, the need for part-time workers
increases.

Shared Time

One particular type of part-time work gaining
popularity today is referred to as job sharing. In job
sharing a full-time position is simply "split in two."[15]
With a shared-time arrangement, the job may be split into a
four or five-hour shift for each worker, or it may be divided into full-time work for each for a certain period of
time--for example, a six-month work period followed by a
six-month free period for each worker.[16]

Job sharing or shared-time work has obvious benefits
for both employers and employees. Employers usually get
more than an eight-hour day out of each shared job without
paying overtime.[17] Also, with the increasing automation of
assembly lines, companies can avoid massive lay-offs by using job sharing.[18] Employees benefit, too, from shared jobs.
Working as a team, many are able to have permanent employ-

ment and still continue their education. Other people who want the security of a full-time position but who are unwilling to work a full seven or eight-hour day find job sharing the perfect solution to their problem. Women, in particular, have opted for job sharing, especially those women who need less than a full-time wage.[19]

Job sharing is particularly popular in California, where various types of labor ranging from clerical and factory work to teaching are being set up as shared jobs. One of the promoters of job sharing, Barry Olmsted, sums up the rationale for this kind of work schedule: "We want to face reality: most jobs are set up on a 40-hour-a-week basis. Job sharing is an effort to plug part-timers into that framework."[20]

Nighttime

Perhaps the most noticeable proof that our country is moving away from the eight- or nine-to-five schedule is the increasing number of people one sees heading for work at odd hours of the evening or night. Alvin Toffler comments that "in the technological nations the number of night workers now runs between 15 and 25 percent of all employees." Manufacturing firms, of course, have long operated 24 hours, using three shifts. But today not only manufacturing but also service and computer-based companies are employing nighttime workers.[21]

The advantages of nighttime work for the person who likes to sleep most of the day are obvious. Night shifts also fit the needs of men and women who must take turns caring for their children; one parent is always at home, eliminating the need for sitters or day-care centers.

Evidence of the New Work Schedules

The new work schedules are apparent in the hours being kept by supermarkets in large cities as well as small towns. The all-night supermarket, once associated only with California, is becoming commonplace throughout the United States.[22] Bankers, too, now offer 24-hour service. And Showtime Television recently announced its new 24-hour programing. The current shopping, banking, and entertainment hours of Americans are simply a reflection of the new work schedules they are following.

Even the traffic flow shows our change from traditional scheduling. As Alvin Toffler puts it: "If traffic flows all day long, as it does in an increasing number of cities, and moves in all directions, rather than merely back and forth, it is safe to assume . . . that flextime has begun to spread, that part-time and night work are prevalent, and that all-night services . . . will not be far behind."[23]

Clearly, the United States in the 1980s is beginning to say a final good-bye to nine-to-five jobs. By the year 2000 less rigid patterns of scheduling seem destined to replace almost entirely the eight- or nine-to-five workday.

Notes

[1]Alvin Toffler, The Third Wave (New York: Bantam Books, 1980), p. 246.

[2]Jonathan Wolman, "Work Place 2000," part 2 of "Working in the Year 2000," Atlanta Journal-Atlanta Constitution, 20 August 1978, Sec. C, p. 8.

[3]Toffler, p. 246.

[4]Lillian Craig Harris, "Work and Leisure: Putting It All Together," Manpower, January 1974, p. 24.

[5]Toffler, pp. 246-47.

[6]Patricia A. Renwick, Edward E. Lawler, and the Psychology Today Staff, "What You Really Want from Your Job," Psychology Today, May 1978, p. 54.

[7]Toffler, p. 247.

[8]William Abbott, "Work in the Year 2001," The Futurist, February 1977, p. 25.

[9]Abbott, p. 25.

[10]Toffler, p. 248.

[11]Wolman, p. 1.

[12]Abbott, p. 29.

[13]Janet Guyon, "The American Workplace," The Wall Street Journal, 29 April 1981, p. 1, col. 3.

[14]Wolman, pp. 1, 8.

[15]Wolman, p. 1.

[16]Les Rich, "Job-Sharing: Another Way to Work," Worklife, May 1978, p. 5.

[17]Wolman, p. 1.

[18]Rich, p. 5.

[19]Rich, pp. 4-5.

[20]Wolman, p. 1.

[21]Toffler, p. 248.

[22]Toffler, p. 249.

[23]Toffler, pp. 250-51.

Bibliography

Abbott, William. "Work in the Year 2001." The Futurist, February 1977, pp. 25-30.

Guyon, Janet. "The American Workplace." The Wall Street Journal, 29 April 1981, p. 1, col. 3.

Harris, Lillian Craig. "Work and Leisure: Putting It All Together." Manpower, January 1974, pp. 22-26.

Renwick, Patricia A., Edward E. Lawler, and the Psychology Today Staff. "What You Really Want from Your Job." Psychology Today, May 1978, pp. 53-65.

Rich, Les. "Job-Sharing: Another Way to Work." Worklife, May 1978, pp. 4-7.

Toffler, Alvin. The Third Wave. New York: Bantam Books, 1980.

Wolman, Jonathan. "Work Place 2000," part 2 of "Working in the Year 2000." Atlanta Journal-Atlanta Constitution, 20 August 1978, Sec. C, pp. 1, 8.

The documented report

NAME _____

DIRECTIONS   Following the pattern illustrated in "No More Nine to Five: The Work Schedules of the Future," prepare a documented report on one of the topics listed below. Use the card catalog and the *Readers' Guide* or the *Social Sciences Index* at your library to locate information about your topic. Try to make use of at least five sources in preparing your report.

SUGGESTED TOPICS

1. A New Fringe Benefit: The Sabbatical
2. The Growing Popularity of Educational Leaves
3. Who's Responsible for the So-called "Work Ethic"?
4. The Effect of Microprocessors on _____ (your field)
5. What's the Right Age for Retirement?
6. Some Problems with Flextime
7. Characteristics of the Workaholic

APPENDIX

Parts of speech	Uses in the sentence	Examples
1. **Verbs**	Indicators of action or state of being (often link subjects and complements)	Tom *hit* the curve. Mary *was* tired. He *is* a senator.
2. **Nouns**	Subjects, objects, complements	*Kay* gave *Ron* the *book* of *poems*. *Jane* is a *student*.
3. **Pronouns**	Substitutes for nouns	*He* will return *it* to *her* later.
4. **Adjectives**	Modifiers of nouns and pronouns	*The long* poem is *the best*.
5. **Adverbs**	Modifiers of verbs, adjectives, adverbs, or whole clauses	sang *loudly* a *very* sad song *entirely too* fast *Indeed*, we will.
6. **Prepositions**	Words used before nouns and pronouns to relate them to other words in the sentence	*to* the lake *in* a hurry *with* no thought *beside* her
7. **Conjunctions**	Words that link words, phrases, or clauses; may be either coordinating or subordinating	win *or* lose in the morning *and* at night We won today, *but* we lost last week. Come *as* you are.
8. **Interjections**	Expressions of emotion (unrelated grammatically to the rest of the sentence)	*Woe* is me! *Ouch!* *Imagine!*

Common auxiliaries (helping verbs)

am	could	have	should
am (is, are, *etc.*)	did	have to	used to
going to OR	do	is	was
about to	does	may	were
are	had	might	will
be	had to	must	would
been	has	ought to	
can	has to	shall	

Forms of the verb *to be*

am	have been	were
are	is	will OR shall be
had been	was	will OR shall have been
has been		

Common indefinite pronouns—*those usually considered singular*

another	each	everything	nothing
anybody	either	neither	one
anyone	everybody	nobody	somebody
anything	everyone	no one	something

—*those considered singular or plural*

all	more	none
any	most	some

Relative pronouns

that	which	whoever	whomever
what	who	whom	whose

Common prepositions

across	between	in regard to	through
after	by	like	to
as	for	near	under
at	from	of	until
because of	in	on	up
before	in front of	over	with
beside			

Subordinating conjunctions (OR *subordinators*)

after	because	so that	when
although	before	that	whenever
as	if	though	where
as if	in order that	unless	wherever
as though	since	until	while

Coordinating conjunctions (OR *coordinators*)

and	nor	yet
but	or	
for	so	

Conjunctive adverbs

accordingly	henceforth	otherwise
also	however	still
anyhow	indeed	then
besides	instead	therefore
consequently	likewise	thus
first, second, third, *etc.*	meanwhile	
furthermore	moreover	
hence	nevertheless	

Common transitional phrases

as a result	in addition	on the other hand
at the same time	in fact	that is
for example	in other words	
for instance	on the contrary	

Principal parts of some troublesome verbs

PRESENT	PAST	PAST PARTICIPLE
begin	began	begun
blow	blew	blown
break	broke	broken
burst	burst	burst
choose	chose	chosen
come	came	come
do	did	done
draw	drew	drawn
drink	drank	drunk
drive	drove	driven
eat	ate	eaten
fly	flew	flown
freeze	froze	frozen
give	gave	given
grow	grew	grown
know	knew	known
lay	laid	laid
lie	lay	lain
raise	raised	raised
ring	rang	rung
rise	rose	risen
run	ran	run
see	saw	seen
set	set	set
sit	sat	sat
speak	spoke	spoken
steal	stole	stolen
swim	swam	swum
take	took	taken
wear	wore	worn
write	wrote	written

Individual Spelling List

In this list write every word that you misspell—in spelling tests (see pages 207–18), in themes, or in any other written work.

WORD (CORRECTLY SPELLED)	WORD (SPELLED BY SYLLABLES) WITH TROUBLE SPOT CIRCLED	REASON FOR ERROR*

*See pages 205–17 for a discussion of the chief reasons for misspelling. Indicate the reason for your misspelling by writing a, b, c, d, e, f, g, or h in this column.

a = Mispronunciation
b = Confusion of words similar in sound
    and/or spelling
c = Error in adding prefix
d = Error in adding suffix

e = Confusion of *ei* and *ie*
f = Error in forming the plural
g = Error in using hyphens
h = Any other reason for misspelling

Individual Spelling List (cont.)

WORD (CORRECTLY SPELLED)	WORD (SPELLED BY SYLLABLES) WITH TROUBLE SPOT CIRCLED	REASON FOR ERROR

Individual Spelling List (cont.)

WORD (CORRECTLY SPELLED)	WORD (SPELLED BY SYLLABLES) WITH TROUBLE SPOT CIRCLED	REASON FOR ERROR

A 2
B 3
C 4
D 5
E 6
F 7
G 8
H 9
I 0
J 1